AMERICA'S
FAMILY
FAVORITES

Best Of
Home
Cooking

AMERICA'S FAMILY FAVORITES

Best Of
Home
Cooking

OVER **150** TIMELESS RECIPES

First published in 2010

ISBN: 978-1-4454-0568-1

Parragon
Queen Street House
4 Queen Street
Bath, BA1 1HE, UK

Printed in China

All recipes herein were prepared and
photographed by John Mitzewich, except
those appearing on pages 29, 49, 53, 59, 61,
69, 73, 97, 115, 125, 127, 245, 257, 265, 301,
305, 309, 313.

Contents

Introduction

There are two kinds of cookbooks – those made for looking, and those made for cooking.

Inspect any kitchen's collection of cookbooks and you'll notice three or four that clearly stand out from the others. They display the obvious signs of regular use: dog-eared pages, scuffed covers, notes scribbled in the margin, and more than a few stains. It's the ultimate goal of this cookbook to become one of those well-worn kitchen companions.

So what do these less-than-mint-condition cookbooks have in common? Generally, they're not written by the world's most famous chefs, don't feature cutting-edge techniques, and certainly aren't exploring the latest culinary trends. No, you probably won't find any of that, but what you will find is lots of what's most commonly referred to as "real food". The kind of hearty, comfort food that makes you glad you're enjoying it around people you love.

Simply put, these cookbooks are where you'll find all those family favorites – a big bowl of spicy chili on a cold, rainy day; the preposterous, yet perfectly delicious Buffalo chicken wings eaten watching football; a plate of warm chocolate chip cookies next to an ice-cold, frosty pitcher of milk.

This cookbook is dedicated to those of you who see no need to reinvent buttermilk biscuits, or deconstruct the venerable tuna noodle casserole. It's written for people that like to understand what they're eating, and who celebrate the time-honored traditions of American cuisine. Cooks who believe meatloaf is always served with mashed potatoes, and that's just the way it is.

This collection of dishes offers a wide array of real American food – from recipes inspired by staples our indigenous tribes shared with the first European settlers, to more whimsical modern takes on kitschy classics. You'll also find some of your favorite restaurant specials redesigned to work in any home kitchen.

Speaking of real food, this book is a bit of a rarity these days, in that all the photos show the actual food the recipes produced. No professional food stylists were used, so what you see is what you get. Besides, these kinds of dishes really don't need to be manipulated. Is there anything more naturally beautiful than a perfectly browned dish of scalloped potatoes, or a freshly baked batch of dusty-topped dinner rolls?

Like American Cookery itself, the recipes in this book aspire to nothing more than tasting great, satisfying your hunger, and making a table full of family feel loved. May it provide many long years of delicious memories – and hopefully, someday it will be one of the worst-looking cookbooks on the shelf.

John Mitzewich

Shrimp Cocktail

Unless you've made one fresh at home from scratch, you've never really had a shrimp cocktail before.

2 lbs jumbo shrimp (12 to 15 per lb), deveined, but unpeeled
1 lemon cut in wedges
1 cup prepared cocktail sauce

For the poaching liquid...
3 quarts cold water
½ onion, sliced
2 garlic cloves, peeled and bruised
2 springs tarragon
1 bay leaf
1 tbsp Old Bay seasoning
½ lemon, juiced
1 tsp black peppercorns

For the cocktail sauce...
½ cup ketchup
¼ cup chili sauce
¼ cup horseradish, or to taste
1 tsp fresh lemon juice
1 tsp Worcestershire sauce
Dash of hot sauce, optional
Pinch of salt

Frozen shrimp are now commonly available deveined (meaning the intestinal track removed), but with the shell on. This style makes the best shrimp cocktail since the shell adds flavor when they are poached.

If you can't find this type, get shell-on shrimp and use a pair of scissors to make a cut through the shell, down the back of the shrimp. Then use a small sharp knife to make ⅛ inch deep incision and remove the intestinal track. Rinse under cold water.

Add all the poaching liquid ingredients to a large stockpot. Place over high heat and bring to a simmer. Turn the heat down to low and simmer for 30 minutes.

Fill a mixing bowl with ice water and set aside. Turn the heat under the poaching liquid to high, and bring to a boil. Add the shrimp and boil for 5 minutes or until cooked through. Transfer the shrimp into the ice water. When cold, drain well, and serve with cocktail sauce and lemon wedges.

The shrimp can be served as is (also known as "peel and eat"), or for a "fancier" presentation, peel for your guests ahead of time and arrange around the rim of a cocktail glass.

For the sauce (makes 1 cup): Combine all ingredients in a small bowl, mix thoroughly, and refrigerate for at least one hour before serving.

Deviled Eggs

Deviled eggs are a kitschy party food favorite. They're fun to make, fun to serve, fun to eat, and even fun to make fun of. It's not a party until a plate of deviled eggs shows up.

12 large eggs
1 tsp white wine vinegar
4 tbsps mayonnaise
½ tsp Dijon mustard
½ tsp horseradish
¼ tsp Worcestershire sauce
½ tsp salt
Dash of Tabasco
Pinch of cayenne
Paprika or more cayenne to garnish
1 tbsp thinly sliced chives

Place the eggs in a single layer in a large saucepan and cover with cold water by one inch. Bring the water to a boil over high heat. Turn off the heat, and cover tightly with the lid, and set a timer for 17 minutes.

Carefully pour off most the hot water, and fill the pan with cold water. Allow to sit for 3 minutes. Pour off most of the water, and again fill the pan with cold water. Leave for 15 minutes. Drain and refrigerate the eggs until needed.

Peel the eggs under cold running water. Cut the eggs in half lengthwise and pop out the yolks into a small mixing bowl. Add the vinegar, mayonnaise, mustard, horseradish, Worcestershire, salt, Tabasco, and cayenne. Mash and mix with a wire whisk until smooth and light.

Using a spoon, or pastry bag with a star tip, fill the egg white halves with the yolk mixture. Sprinkle tops with paprika or cayenne. Chill before serving with the sliced chives.

Makes 24

Maryland Crab Cakes with Tartar Sauce

Contrary to what you get at most restaurants, the main ingredient in crab cakes should be...crab! If you're going to splurge, the last thing you want is a bunch of filler getting in the way.

1 large egg, beaten
2 tbsps mayonnaise
½ tsp Dijon mustard
¼ tsp Worcestershire sauce
½ tsp Old Bay seasoning
¼ tsp salt, or to taste
Pinch of cayenne pepper, optional
1 lb fresh lump crabmeat, well drained
10 saltine crackers
Plain breadcrumbs, as needed
1 tbsp vegetable oil
2 tbsps unsalted butter

For the Tartar Sauce...
1 cup mayonnaise
¼ cup sweet pickle relish
1 tbsp very finely minced onion
1 tbsp chopped capers
1 tbsp chopped parsley
1½ tbsps freshly squeezed lemon juice
Dash of Worcestershire sauce
Few drops of Tabasco, optional
Salt and fresh ground black pepper to taste

Add the egg, mayonnaise, mustard, Worcestershire, Old Bay, salt, and cayenne to a mixing bowl. Whisk together to combine. Crush the saltine crackers into very fine crumbs and add to the bowl. Stir with a spatula until combined. Let sit for 5 minutes.

Gently fold in the crabmeat. Mix with a spatula just enough to combine ingredients. Try not to mash the crab any more than necessary. Cover the bowl and refrigerate for at least 1 hour.

Sprinkle the breadcrumbs on a large plate until lightly covered. Shape the crab mixture into 6 evenly sized cakes, about an inch thick, and place on the plate as they are formed. Dust the tops of each crab cake lightly with more breadcrumbs.

Note: Real American crab cakes are almost all crab, which makes them very fragile to handle. As long as they hold together enough to get into the pan, they will bind together as the egg cooks, and golden-brown crust forms.

Heat the vegetable oil and butter in a large skillet over medium-high heat. When the foam from the butter begins to dissipate, carefully transfer each crab cake from the plate to the pan, using a heatproof spatula.

Sauté until golden brown, about 4 minutes per side. Drain on a paper towel, and serve garnished with remoulade, cocktail sauce or a squeeze of lemon.

For the sauce: Mix together all the ingredients in a bowl. Season with salt and fresh ground black pepper to taste. Best if refrigerated at least an hour before serving. Makes about 1½ cups.

Clams Casino

This is simply the best clam recipe ever. Whenever bacon and butter appear in the same recipe, you know you're in for a treat! Ironically, I've never eaten these in a casino.

18 medium-sized (about 2½ inches)
of littleneck clams
2 tbsps unsalted butter
3 strips center-cut bacon, each sliced
into 6 equal pieces (18 total)
3 tbsps finely diced red bell pepper
3 garlic cloves, finely minced
⅓ cup plain breadcrumbs
1 tbsp finely grated Parmesan
⅛ tsp freshly ground black pepper
Pinch of salt
2 tbsps chopped flat leaf parsley
Lemon wedges
Rock salt as needed

Heat butter in a skillet over medium heat. Add the bacon and sauté until cooked, but not quite crisp. Using a slotted spoon, transfer the bacon to a plate and reserve.

Add the red pepper to the bacon drippings in the skillet, and cook for 2 minutes. Add the garlic and cook for 1 minute more. Turn off the heat and stir in the breadcrumbs, Parmesan, black pepper, and salt. Reserve the mixture until needed.

Add about 2 inches of water to a Dutch oven, or other heavy pot with a tight-fitting lid, and bring to a rapid boil over high heat. Add clams, cover, and cook for about 5 minutes, or just until the shells open. It's critical to remove and drain the clams as soon as they open. Allow the clams to cool until they can be handled.

Twist and pull the clamshells apart, and remove the clam. Place the clam back into the deeper of the two shell halves. Spread the rock salt on a heatproof baking dish, and set the clams on top of the salt, pressing in slightly.

Divide the breadcrumb mixture evenly over the top of each clamshell, and top with one piece of bacon. Broil on high, about 8 inches from the heat, until the tops are browned and the edges of the bacon are crisp. Sprinkle on the fresh parsley, and serve hot with lemon wedges.

Buffalo Chicken Wings

America's favorite appetizer is usually deep fried, but this delicious home version uses a very hot oven instead.

4 lbs chicken wings
1 tbsp vegetable oil
1 tbsp all-purpose flour
1 tsp salt

For the sauce...
⅔ cup Frank's Louisiana hot sauce
1 stick (½ cup) cold unsalted butter, cut into 1 inch slices
1½ tbsps white vinegar
¼ tsp Worcestershire sauce
1 tsp Tabasco
¼ tsp cayenne pepper
⅛ tsp garlic powder
Salt to taste

Pre-heat oven to 425°F.

If the chicken wings being used were frozen and thawed, be sure they're completely dry before starting recipe. If using whole wings, cut each into two pieces (in wing-speak called the "flat" and the "drum"). The small wing tips can be discarded, or saved for stock. In a large mixing bowl, toss the wings with the oil, salt, and flour until evenly coated

Line two heavy-duty baking sheets with lightly greased foil, or silicon baking mats. Divide the wings and spread out evenly. Do not crowd. Bake for 25 minutes, remove, and turn the wings over. Return to the oven and cook another 20 to 30 minutes, or until the wings are well-browned and cooked through

Note: Cooking times will vary based on size of the wings. When fully cooked, the bones will easily pull out from the meat.

While the wings are baking, mix all the sauce ingredients in a saucepan. Bring to a simmer, whisking, over medium heat. Remove from heat and reserve. Taste sauce; adjust for salt and spiciness, if desired.

After the wings are cooked, transfer to a large mixing bowl. Pour the warm sauce over the hot wings and toss with a spoon or spatula to completely coat. Let rest 5 minutes, toss again, and serve immediately with celery sticks and blue cheese dressing on the side.

Makes 40

Sticky Ginger Garlic Wings

Asian-flavored chicken wings now rival the venerable Buffalo-style in popularity, and this sticky, spicy, garlicky version is my favorite.

4 lbs chicken wings
1 tbsp vegetable oil
1 tbsp all-purpose flour
1 tsp salt

For the Sticky Ginger Garlic Sauce...
4 crushed garlic cloves, peeled, finely minced
2 tbsps freshly grated ginger root
¼ tsp hot pepper flakes, or to taste
½ cup rice vinegar
½ cup packed dark brown sugar
1 tsp soy sauce

Pre-heat oven to 425°F.

If the chicken wings being used were frozen and thawed, be sure they're completely dry before starting recipe. If using whole wings, cut each into two pieces (in wing-speak called the "flat" and the "drum"). The small wing tips can be discarded, or saved for stock. In a large mixing bowl, toss the wings with the oil and salt. Add the flour and toss until evenly coated.

Line two heavy-duty baking sheets with lightly greased foil, or silicon baking mats. Divide the wings and spread out evenly. Do not crowd. Bake for 25 minutes, remove, and turn the wings over. Return to the oven and cook another 20 to 30 minutes, or until the wings are well-browned and cooked through.

Note: Cooking times will vary based on size of the wings. When fully cooked, the bones will easily pull out from the meat.

While the wings are baking, mix all the sauce ingredients in a saucepan. Bring to a simmer, whisking, over medium heat. Remove from heat and reserve.

After the wings are cooked, transfer to a large mixing bowl. Pour the warm sauce over the hot wings and toss with a spoon or spatula to completely coat. Let rest 10 minutes, and toss again. The glaze will get sticky and thicken slightly as is cools.

Serve warm or room temperature.

Guacamole

Guacamole, chips, and fresh salsa – the cornerstone of any great party's snack table.

6 ripe avocados, halved, pitted
4 green onions, light parts only, finely diced
1 jalapeno pepper, seeded, finely diced
⅓ cup chopped fresh cilantro
3 tbsps freshly squeezed lime juice
1½ tsp salt, or to taste
Cayenne to taste

Scoop the avocados into a bowl. Add the rest of the ingredients and mash with a potato masher or fork as smooth or chunky as you like. Best if chilled for 30 minutes before serving.

Serves 12

Fresh Tomato Salsa

The sooner you learn that your party is only as good as the salsa, the better.

2 cups diced vine ripe red tomatoes
½ cup diced red bell pepper
¼ cup diced red onion
¼ cup diced white onion
1 clove garlic, minced
2 jalapeno peppers, seeded, white membrane removed, diced fine
2 tbsps fresh lime juice
1 tbsp vegetable oil
¼ tsp chipotle pepper
Pinch of dried oregano
¼ tsp sugar
½ tsp salt, or to taste
½ bunch fresh cilantro, chopped

In a large, non-reactive bowl, combine all the ingredients and mix well. Chill for an hour before serving. Best if used within eight hours of being made.

Makes 3 cups

Hot Spinach Artichoke Dip

This warm, savory dip is fast to make, and a proven crowd-pleaser. Great with chips, but even better on freshly sliced French bread. This slightly healthier version omits the usual addition of mayonnaise with no ill effects.

2 tbsps butter
½ cup chopped green onions, white and light green parts only
Pinch of salt
2 cloves garlic, very finely minced
1 package (10 oz) frozen chopped spinach, thawed, drained, squeezed dry
1 can (14 oz) artichoke hearts, drained, roughly chopped
8 oz cream cheese
¼ cup sour cream
¼ tsp hot sauce
Very small pinch of nutmeg
½ cup grated Parmesan cheese, preferably Parmigiano Reggiano
¼ cup mozzarella, grated

Pre-heat oven to 400°F.

Sauté the onions with a pinch of salt in the butter over medium heat until translucent. Add the garlic, stir to combine, and immediately turn off the heat; reserve.

In a mixing bowl, combine the spinach, artichoke hearts, cream cheese, sour cream, Mozzarella cheese, hot sauce, nutmeg, and Parmesan cheese. Add the onion mixture, and stir until thoroughly mixed.

Transfer the mixture into a small baking dish, and top with the mozzarella. Bake until bubbling and golden, about 25 minutes. The dip may be placed under a hot broiler for a few minutes, if a browner top is desired.

Oyster Rockefeller

The original recipe for this baked oyster dish is a guarded secret of Antoine's, New Orleans' oldest Creole restaurant, but many versions have been created. Spinach features in most.

24 large live oysters
Rock salt
3 tbsps butter
6 scallions, chopped
1 large garlic clove, crushed
3 tbsps finely chopped celery
1½ oz watercress sprigs
1¾ cups young spinach leaves, rinsed and any tough stems removed
1 tbsp anise-flavored liqueur, such as Anisette or Pastis
4 tbsps fresh bread crumbs
Few drops of hot pepper sauce, to taste
Salt and pepper
Lemon wedges, to serve

Pre-heat oven to 400°F.

Shuck the oysters, running an oyster knife under each oyster to loosen it from its shell. Pour off the liquor. Arrange a ½ to ¾ inch layer of salt in a roasting pan large enough to hold the oysters in a single layer, or use 2 roasting pans. Nestle the oyster shells in the salt so that they remain upright. Cover with a thick, damp dish towel and let chill while you make the topping.

If you don't have oyster plates with indentations that hold the shells upright, line 4 plates with a layer of salt deep enough to hold six shells upright. Set the plates aside.

Melt half the butter in a large skillet over medium heat. Add the scallions, garlic, and celery and cook, stirring frequently, for 2 to 3 minutes until softened.

Stir in the remaining butter, then add the watercress and spinach and cook, stirring constantly, for 1 minute, or until the leaves wilt. Transfer to a blender or small food processor and add the liqueur, bread crumbs, hot pepper sauce, and salt and pepper to taste. Whiz until well blended.

Spoon 2 to 3 tsps of the sauce over each oyster. Bake in the oven for 20 minutes. Transfer to the prepared plates and serve with lemon wedges.

Cook's tip: The exact amount of sauce needed depends on the size of the oysters - this is enough to top 24 large oysters. Any leftovers can be stirred into vegetable soups, or mixed with mayonnaise to make a sauce for sandwiches.

Serves 4

Chorizo & Cheese Quesadillas with Chipotle Sour Cream

Quesadillas are such a great party food – fast, easy, and a proven crowd-pleaser.

4 oz mozzarella cheese grated
4 oz cheddar cheese grated
8 oz chorizo sausage (outer case removed)
or ham diced
4 scallions, finely chopped
2 fresh green chilies seeded and chopped
8 flour Tortillas
Vegetable oil for brushing
Salt and pepper to taste
Lime wedges to garnish

For the sour cream...
1 cup sour cream
1 tbsp minced canned chipotles in adobo
sauce or ¾ tsp chipotle powder, or to taste

Place the cheese, chorizo, scallions, chillies, salt and pepper in a bowl and mix together.

Divide the mixture between 4 of the flour tortillas, then top with the remaining tortillas.

Brush a large, non-stick or heavy-bottom skillet with oil and heat over medium heat. Add 1 quesadilla and cook, pressing it down with a spatula, for 4 to 5 minutes until the underside is crisp and lightly browned. Turn over and cook the other side until the cheese is melting. Remove from the skillet and keep warm. Cook the remaining quesadillas.

Cut each one into quarters , arrange on a warmed serving plate and serve accompanied by some Guacamole or Salsa.

In a medium bowl, combine the sour cream and chipotles. Whisk together to fully incorporate.

Serves 4

Crispy Chicken Fingers with Honey Mustard Dip

Millions of kids can't be wrong – crispy chicken fingers rule! Make a batch of these and see what a certain "nugget" of chicken is really supposed to taste like.

4 large skinless, boneless chicken breasts, cut into ½ inch strips
1 cup all-purpose flour
2 tsps salt
1 tsp garlic salt
1 tsp chipotle pepper
½ tsp white pepper
4 eggs, beaten
1 tbsp milk
3 cups Japanese-style panko bread crumbs
Canola oil for frying

For the sauce...
½ cup mayonnaise
2 tbsps Dijon mustard
2 tbsps yellow mustard
1 tbsp rice vinegar
2 tbsps honey
½ tsp hot sauce, optional

Add the flour, salt, garlic salt, chipotle, and white pepper into a large, sealable plastic freezer bag. Shake to mix. Add the chicken strips, seal the bag, and shake vigorously to coat evenly with flour.

In a mixing bowl, whisk together the egg and milk. Add the chicken strips, shaking off the excess flour as you remove them from the bag. Stir until the strips are completely coated in the egg.

Pour the breadcrumbs in a shallow pan. Use one hand (called the "wet" hand) to remove the chicken strips from the bowl of eggs, a few at a time, allowing the excess egg to drip off, and place in the pan of panko. Use the other hand (called the "dry" hand) to coat the chicken in the breadcrumbs, pressing them in firmly. As they are breaded, place the strips on baking sheets or racks. When done breading let the chicken strips rest for 10 to 15 minutes before frying.

Pour about ½ inch of oil in a large, heavy skillet (ideally cast iron) and set over medium high heat. When the oil is hot enough to fry (350°F to 375°F or test with a small piece of breading), cook for 2 to 3 minutes per side, or until golden brown and cooked through. Work in batches, drain on paper towels or baking rack, and keep the cooked chicken fingers in a warm oven (175°F) until the rest are done.

To make the honey mustard sauce combine all the ingredients and mix well. Serve immediately.

Serves 8

Waldorf Salad

It's amazing how such a simple list of ingredients can come together to create such a delicious and complexly flavored salad. This sweet, crunchy classic is named for the Waldorf Astoria Hotel in New York City, where it was first created.

¾ cup raw walnut halves
3 apples, cored, cut into 1 inch chunks
1 cup green or red seedless grape halves
⅔ cup sliced celery, about ¼ inch thick
⅓ cup mayonnaise
2 tbsps freshly squeezed lemon juice
1 tbsp plain yogurt
½ tsp salt
Fresh ground black pepper to taste
1 small head butter lettuce

Pre-heat oven to 350°F.

Arrange walnuts on a baking sheet, and bake for 8 minutes. Let cool on a cutting board, roughly chop, and reserve.

Add the mayonnaise, lemon juice, yogurt, salt, and a few grinds of black pepper to a large mixing bowl. Whisk to combine thoroughly. Use a spatula to fold in the apples, grapes, celery, and walnuts. Mix until evenly coated with the dressing.

Lay down a few lettuce leaves on each plate and spoon the Waldorf salad over the top. Serve immediately.

Note: Try and use three different varieties of apple for an even more interesting salad.

Cobb Salad

America's most famous "composed" salad was invented at Los Angeles' Brown Derby restaurant in 1937. The ingredients are traditionally arranged in neat rows on top of the greens, but if you don't want to bother, it's just as delicious with everything tossed together.

8 slices bacon
4 large handfuls mixed baby greens,
or other lettuce, torn into bite-size pieces
3 hard-boiled eggs, peeled, chopped
4 cups cooked chicken, cubed
2 avocados, peeled, pitted, cubed
1 cup cherry tomatoes, halved
4 oz Roquefort cheese, crumbled
½ tsp Dijon mustard
¼ cup red wine vinegar
1 tsp Worcestershire sauce
1 clove garlic, crushed into a paste
¼ tsp salt
¼ tsp fresh ground black pepper
⅓ cup olive oil

Cook the bacon until crisp, drain on paper towels, and when cool enough to handle, crumble and set aside.

Arrange a bed of lettuce in shallow bowls. Arrange the eggs, bacon, chicken, avocados, tomatoes, and Roquefort cheese in rows on top of the lettuce, covering the surface completely.

In a bowl, whisk together the mustard, vinegar, Worcestershire, garlic, salt, and pepper. Slowly drizzle in the olive oil, whisking constantly, to form the dressing.

Drizzle the dressing evenly over the salad, and serve immediately.

Serves 4

Roasted Red Potato Salad

*This salad will look so tasty you'll want to dive right in, but be sure to wait
at least two hours to give the flavors a chance to develop fully.*

2½ lbs small red potatoes, washed
Salt to taste
2 cloves garlic, finely minced
1 tsp Dijon mustard
Pinch of cayenne
¼ cup white wine vinegar
1 tbsp chopped Italian parsley
1 tbsp chopped tarragon
1 tbsp chopped chives
1 tsp minced thyme leaves
⅔ cup olive oil
Freshly ground black pepper to taste

Pre-heat oven to 400°F.

Place the potatoes in a roasting pan. Bake for 25 to 30 minutes, or until tender (time will vary depending on size).

While the potatoes are in the oven, make the dressing. Add the garlic, Dijon, cayenne, and vinegar to a large mixing bowl. Whisk in the oil, very slowly at first, in a steady stream until incorporated.

When the cooked potatoes are just cool enough to handle, cut in halves or quarters. Add and toss the warm potatoes in the dressing, along with salt and fresh ground black pepper to taste. Let sit for 15 minutes. Add the herbs and toss again.

Cover and refrigerate for at least 2 hours or overnight. Toss well before serving, and taste for salt and pepper. Additional fresh herbs can be sprinkled over the top if desired.

Serves 6

Potato and Egg Salad

If you find yourself at a summer picnic, and there isn't a big bowl of this salad there, leave immediately.

4 lbs russet potatoes, peeled, quartered
3 hard-boiled eggs, chopped
1 cup diced celery
⅓ cup minced green onions,
white and light green parts only
1¼ cup mayonnaise
2 tbsps cider vinegar
1 tbsp Dijon mustard
1½ tsps salt
½ tsp sugar
¼ tsp freshly ground black pepper
⅛ tsp cayenne, optional

Boil potatoes in salted water until just tender, drain well, and let cool to room temperature. Cut into 1 inch pieces and add to a large bowl. Add the eggs and celery.

In a small mixing bowl combine the rest of the ingredients. Pour over the potato mixture, and use a spatula to thoroughly combine.

Chill in the refrigerator for at least one hour before serving.

Deli-Style Macaroni Salad

Take your time, and use your sharpest knife to get a nice fine dice on the veggies in this classic pasta salad. When made right, this is a macaroni salad where every forkful bursts with flavor.

1 lb dry elbow macaroni, cooked, rinsed in cold water, and drained well

For the dressing...
1½ cups mayonnaise
½ cup sour cream
2 tbsps cider vinegar
1 tbsp Dijon mustard
1 tsp sugar
½ cup finely diced celery
¼ cup minced red onion
½ cup sweet pickle relish
¼ finely grated carrot
2 tbsps finely diced red bell pepper
¼ cup chopped parsley
½ tsp freshly ground black pepper
1½ tsps salt, or to taste

Whisk together all the dressing ingredients in a large mixing bowl, and add the drained pasta. Toss to combine thoroughly. Refrigerate for at least 2 hours before serving.

Note: Some of the minced vegetables can be reserved to scatter over the top for a more colorful presentation.

Serves 8

Caesar Salad with Homemade Garlic Croutons

As the story goes, America's most popular restaurant salad was invented in 1924 by Caesar Cardini in Tijuana, Mexico. It's a masterpiece of taste and texture, made more so by homemade garlic croutons.

For the dressing...
2 egg yolks, from coddled eggs
2 large garlic cloves, minced
3 whole anchovy fillets
¾ cup mayonnaise
½ cup finely grated Parmigiano-Reggiano
Parmesan cheese
⅓ cup olive oil
¼ cup freshly squeezed lemon juice
1 tbsp cold water
1 tsp freshly ground black pepper, or to taste
Salt to taste

For the salads...
6 hearts of romaine lettuce, torn or cut into
2 inch pieces, washed, dried thoroughly
¾ cup Caesar dressing, more as needed
4 cups Garlic Parmesan Croutons
1 cup shaved Parmesan cheese,
more as needed
Freshly ground black pepper, to taste

For the garlic croutons...
4 cloves garlic, minced very fine
½ cup olive oil
1 (8 oz) loaf French baguette or similar style
bread (for best results, use day old bread)
¾ cup finely grated "real" Parmesan cheese
(sold as Parmigiano-Reggiano)
½ tsp dried Italian herbs
½ tsp paprika
½ tsp salt
½ tsp freshly ground black pepper
Pinch of cayenne

For the dressing: To coddle eggs: Place 2 room temperature eggs in a small saucepan. Pour in boiling water until the eggs are covered. Leave for 1 minute, then drain and run under cold water until the eggs are cool enough to be handled. When cool separate the eggs and reserve the yolks.

Add the rest of the dressing ingredients to a blender, along with the egg yolks. Blend until smooth. Refrigerate until needed.

For the salads: Combine the romaine, croutons, and dressing in a large mixing bowl. Toss with tongs until the lettuce is completely coated with dressing. Divide onto chilled plates and top with the shaved Parmesan (a potato peeler works best for this), and freshly ground black pepper to taste. Serve immediately with extra dressing on the side.

For the croutons: Pre-heat oven to 300°F.

Slightly crush the garlic, combine with the olive oil in a small mixing bowl and let sit for 4 hours. Cut the bread into 1 inch cubes and add to mixing bowl. Add ½ cup cheese, dried herbs, paprika, salt, black pepper and cayenne. Strain the garlic oil over the bread cubes but throw away the crushed garlic cloves. Mix thoroughly. Put the mixture on a baking sheet and cook for 15 minutes.

Remove and turn the bread cubes over and return for another 15 minutes. Remove and sprinkle with the remaining cheese and return to the oven for final 15 minutes until brown and crunchy.

Scatter over salad or store in airtight container.

Southwest Corn Salad

This cool, colorful, and crunchy salad is perfect when fresh corn is in season, and you want to bring something fabulous to that summer cookout. Frozen corn may be used, but the salad just won't have that same sweet, crisp snap.

3 tbsps olive oil
3 cups fresh corn kernels, about 6 ears
1 (15 oz) can black beans, well rinsed and drained
1 red bell pepper, diced small
1 orange bell pepper, diced small
1 jalapeno pepper, seeded, minced
4 thinly sliced green onions
1 clove garlic, crushed, finely minced
2 tbsps chopped cilantro leaves
½ tsp ground cumin
¼ tsp chipotle pepper, or to taste
3 tbsps fresh lime juice
1 tbsp rice vinegar
1 tsp sugar
1 tsp salt

Heat the olive oil in a large nonstick pan over medium-high heat. Add the corn and sauté, stirring, for about 3 to 4 minutes.

Turn off the pan and transfer corn into a large mixing bowl. Add the rest of the ingredients and toss to combine thoroughly.

Refrigerate for at least 4 hours before serving. Toss well, and taste and adjust for salt and spice before serving.

Serves 6-8

Three Bean Salad

Nothing says summer days more than a lovely light, bright green bean salad.
This easy to make recipe is delicious and quick.

6 oz mixed salad leaves, such as spinach, arrugala and frisée
1 red onion
3 oz radishes
6 oz cherry tomatoes
4 oz cooked beetroot
10 oz canned cannellini beans, drained and rinsed
7 oz canned red kidney beans, drained and rinsed
10½ oz canned flageolet beans, drained and rinsed
1½ oz dried cranberries
2 oz roasted cashew nuts
8 oz feta cheese (drained weight), crumbled

For the dressing...
4 tbsps extra virgin olive oil
1 tsp Dijon mustard
2 tbsps lemon juice
1 tbsp chopped fresh coriander
Salt and pepper

Thinly slice the onion, then cut in half to form half moons and put into a bowl.

Thinly slice the radishes, cut the tomatoes in half and peel the beetroot and add to the onion. Add all remaining ingredients with exception of the nuts and cheese.

To make the dressing, put all the ingredients into a screw-top jar and shake until well-blended.

Pour the dressing over the bean mixture, toss lightly, then spoon on top of the salad leaves. Scatter with the nuts and cheese and serve immediately.

Serves 4-6

Easy Gazpacho

America's favorite cold soup is fast to make, and really hits the spot on those hot summer afternoons.

1 small cucumber, peeled and chopped
2 red bell peppers, seeded and chopped
2 green bell peppers, seeded and chopped
2 garlic cloves, coarsely chopped
1 fresh basil sprig
2½ cups strained tomatoes
1 tbsp extra-virgin olive oil
1 tbsp red wine vinegar
1 tbsp balsamic vinegar
1¼ cups vegetable stock
2 tbsps lemon juice
Salt and pepper

To serve...
2 tbsps diced, peeled cucumber
2 tbsps finely chopped red onion
2 tbsps finely chopped red bell pepper
2 tbsps finely chopped green bell pepper
Ice cubes
4 fresh basil sprigs
Fresh crusty bread

Put the cucumber, bell peppers, garlic, and basil in a food processor and process for 1½ minutes. Add the strained tomatoes, olive oil, and both kinds of vinegar and process until smooth.

Pour in the vegetable stock and lemon juice and stir. Transfer the mixture to a large bowl. Season to taste with salt and pepper. Cover with plastic wrap and let chill in the refrigerator for at least 2 hours.

To serve, prepare the cucumber, onion, and bell peppers, then place in small serving dishes or arrange decoratively on a plate. Place ice cubes in 4 large soup bowls. Stir the soup and ladle it into the bowls. Garnish with the basil sprigs and serve with the prepared vegetables and chunks of fresh crusty bread.

Note: The sweetness of basil works well with this soup, but cilantro is traditional and also very nice.

Serves 4

Split Pea with Ham

One of the easiest soups ever, this split pea recipe gets its deep, rustic flavor from smoked pork hocks. A little fresh ground black pepper is the only garnish you'll need.

2 smoked pork hocks
2 tbsps butter
1 onion, diced
2 ribs celery, diced
3 cloves minced garlic
8 oz diced ham
1 bay leaf
1 lb split peas, rinsed, drained
1 quart chicken broth
3 cups water
Salt and freshly ground black pepper to taste

Melt the butter in a soup pot over medium heat. Add the onion, celery, garlic, and pinch of salt. Cook, stirring, for about 3 minutes. Add the pork hocks, bay leaf, chicken broth, and water. Bring to a simmer, cover, turn heat to low, and cook for 1½ hours.

Add the split peas, cover and continue to cook on low, stirring occasionally for another 1 to 1½ hours, or until the peas are tender, and the soup has thickened. Additional water or broth can be added if the soup is getting too thick for your liking.

Remove the pork hocks, and when cool enough to handle, slice off any meat and add back to the soup (optional). Season with salt and fresh ground black pepper to taste, and serve hot with crackers.

Cream of Mushroom Soup

The secret to this delicious soup is patience. The longer you cook and caramelize the mushrooms in the butter, the deeper and "meatier" the flavor will be. Take your time, flip through a magazine, enjoy the aromas, and you'll be richly rewarded.

¼ cup unsalted butter
2 lbs white or brown button mushrooms, sliced
1 yellow onion, diced
1 tbsp flour
6 sprigs fresh thyme, tied into a bundle with kitchen string, plus some picked leaves to garnish
3 cloves garlic, peeled, left whole
4 cups chicken broth or stock
1 cup water
1 cup heavy cream
Salt and fresh ground black pepper to taste

Melt the butter in a large heavy-bottomed soup pot over medium heat. Add the mushrooms and a big pinch of salt. Cook, stirring often, for 20 to 30 minutes, or until the mushrooms are golden brown. At first, the mushrooms will give up lots of water and simply boil, but as the liquid evaporates, they will start to brown and caramelize.

Note: At this point, you can reserve some of the browned mushrooms to garnish the soup later.

Once the mushrooms are beautifully browned, add the onions and cook over medium-low heat for about 5 more minutes. Add a tbsp of flour and cook, stirring, for 1 minute. Whisk in the chicken broth and water. Add the thyme and garlic, and bring to a simmer. Reduce the heat to low, cover, and simmer gently for 1 hour.

Turn off heat, uncover, and allow to cool for 15 minutes. Carefully puree the soup (in small batches!) in a blender until very smooth. To be safe, place a kitchen towel over the blender, and pulse on and off to begin.

Pour soup back into the pot, and stir in the cream (more broth or water can be added to adjust the thickness if desired). Bring back to a simmer, and season with salt and fresh ground black pepper to taste.

Serve hot, topped with the reserved mushrooms and thyme leaves.

Serves 4

Spiced Pumpkin Soup

Sure pumpkin pie gets all the press, but this great gourd also make a wonderful soup.

2 tbsps olive oil
1 onion, chopped
1 garlic clove, chopped
1 tbsp chopped fresh ginger
1 small red chile, seeded and finely chopped
2 tbsps chopped fresh cilantro
1 bay leaf
2 lbs pumpkin, peeled, seeded diced
2½ cups vegetable stock
Salt and pepper
Light cream, to garnish

Heat the oil in a soup pot over medium heat. Add the onion and garlic and cook, stirring, for about 4 minutes, until slightly softened. Add the ginger, chile, cilantro, bay leaf, and pumpkin, and cook for another 3 minutes.

Pour in the stock and bring to a boil. Using a spoon, skim any foam from the surface. Reduce the heat and simmer gently, stirring occasionally, for about 25 minutes, or until the pumpkin is tender. Remove from the heat, take out the bay leaf, and let cool a little.

Transfer the soup into a food processor or blender and process until smooth (you may have to do this in batches). Return the mixture to the pan and season to taste with salt and pepper.

Reheat gently, stirring. Remove from the heat, pour into warmed soup bowls, garnish each one with a swirl of cream, and serve.

Serves 4

New England Clam Chowder

America's most famous soup features one of the great flavor combinations of all time: bacon, clams and potatoes. This traditional recipe is much lighter in texture than the super thick modern versions you may be used to.

1 lb little neck clams, washed
1 cup water
2 slices bacon, cut into ¼ inch pieces
½ yellow onion, diced
1 tbsp butter
2 tbsps flour
2 (10 oz) cans whole clams, drained
2 cups cold clam juice (note part of this may be made up from the drained canned clam liquid, but clam juice has a stronger clam flavor)
1½ lbs Russet potatoes, peeled, and cut into ¼ inch cubes
1 cup milk
1 cup cream
Salt and freshly ground black pepper to taste
Fresh chopped parsley to garnish
Oyster cracker to garnish

Bring one cup of water to a boil in a small saucepan over high heat. Add the little neck clams, cover tightly, and cook for a couple minutes, until the clams open. Remove the clams to a bowl and reserve. Strain the cooking liquid and reserve.

In large saucepan, over medium heat, cook the bacon in the butter until almost crisp. Remove the bacon with slotted spoon and reserve, leaving the butter and rendered bacon fat in the pan.

Reduce the heat to medium-low, and add the onions. Sauté until soft and translucent, about 5 minutes. Add the flour and cook, stirring, for 2 minutes. Whisk in the cold clam juice, slowly at first. Add the reserved clam cooking liquid. Bring back to a simmer and add the potatoes. Cover and cook for 20 minutes, or until the potatoes are tender.

Note: At this point some chowder-heads like to smash some of the potatoes against the bottom of the pan with a masher to add body to the soup. Optional!

Stir in the canned clams, milk, and cream. Reduce heat to low, and cook until just heated through. Do not boil. Add the reserved little neck clams, and cook for another minute. Taste and season with salt and freshly ground black pepper as needed.

Serve hot topped with the reserved bacon, parsley, and oyster crackers.

Garden Vegetable Soup

This recipe is great as is, but if you're in the mood for something more substantial, you can add some macaroni for a quick and delicious minestrone, or toss in some leftover roast chicken for an even heartier potage.

2 tbsps olive oil
1 yellow onion, diced
2 ribs celery, sliced into ¼ inch pieces
3 carrots, peeled, cut into ½ inch pieces
2 cloves garlic, finely minced
6 cups chicken or vegetable broth
¼ tsp dried thyme
¼ tsp dried basil
2 cups cubed zucchini
1 cup corn kernels
1 can (15 oz) navy beans, drained, rinsed
1 cup cherry tomato halves
1 large handful baby spinach leaves
¼ cup chopped fresh Italian parsley leaves
Salt and fresh ground black pepper to taste

Heat the olive oil in a soup pot over medium-low heat. Add the onions, celery, carrots, and garlic, and a big pinch of salt. Cook, stirring occasionally, until they begin to soften, about 10 minutes.

Add the broth, thyme, and basil; turn up heat to high, and bring to a simmer. Turn down to medium-low and cook for 10 minutes. Add the zucchini, corn, and navy beans. Cover and simmer for 15 minutes, or until the vegetables are tender.

Add the tomatoes, spinach, and parsley. As soon as the spinach wilts, turn off the heat. Season with salt and fresh ground black pepper to taste.

Serve immediately.

Cream of Tomato Soup

Rumor has it this easy soup goes really, really well with toasted cheese sandwiches.

2 tbsps unsalted butter
1 medium sweet onion, coarsely chopped
1 clove garlic, halved
1 (28 oz) can whole, peeled,
Italian plum tomatoes
2 cups chicken broth
½ cup water
1 tsp sugar
1 bay leaf
½ cup heavy cream, divided
Salt and freshly ground black pepper to taste
1 tbsp freshly sliced chives

Melt butter in a saucepan over medium heat. Add the onion with a pinch of salt. Cook, stirring occasionally, for about 10 to 12 minutes until the onion is soft and golden. Add tomatoes (do not drain) to the saucepan and use a wooden spoon, or potato masher to break into large chunks. Add the garlic, sugar, bay leaf, chicken broth, and water; bring up to a simmer. Simmer for 30 minutes.

Remove from heat, and take out the bay leaf. Carefully puree the soup in small batches in a blender until very smooth. Strain the soup back into the saucepan; place over medium-low heat, and bring back to a simmer. Add the cream, reserving 2 to 3 tbsps for the garnish, and stir to combine. Season with salt and freshly ground black pepper to taste.

Place the remaining heavy cream in a small mixing bowl and whisk vigorously for 1 minute or until slightly thickened and frothy. Ladle the hot soup into bowls, and drizzle over some of the whipped cream.

Garnish with chives and serve immediately.

Mom's Chicken Noodle Soup

You know that popular book that was supposed to be like chicken soup for the soul? This really is chicken soup for the soul.

For the broth...
1 large whole chicken, about 4 to 5 lbs
Salt and fresh ground black pepper to taste
1 carrot, chopped
1 rib celery, chopped
1 onion, chopped
1 clove garlic, peeled
4 sprigs thyme
1 bay leaf
1 whole clove
1 tsp ketchup

For the soup...
1 tbsp butter
1 onion, diced
1 cup diced carrots
1 cup diced celery
¼ tsp poultry seasoning
2 cups uncooked egg noodles,
or other macaroni
1 tbsp chopped parsley

Pre-heat oven to 450°F.

Season the chicken inside and out with salt and pepper. Add the carrots, celery and onions to an oiled 9 x 13 inch roasting pan, and place the chicken on top. Roast for 60 minutes, or until a thermometer inserted in the thickest part of a thigh registers 160°F.

Remove the chicken from the oven and allow to rest until cool enough to handle. Pull off the breast meat, and larger pieces of thigh and leg meat, and refrigerate until needed.

Transfer the chicken carcass and vegetables from the roasting pan into a large stockpot. Add 2 quarts of cold water, along with the garlic, thyme, bay leaf, clove, and ketchup. Bring to a boil, turn down heat to low, and simmer for 2 hours. The liquid level should remain about the same, so every so often add a splash of water to the pot.

While the broth is simmering, place a soup pot on medium-low heat. Sauté the diced onion, carrots, and celery in the butter until they begin to soften, about 15 minutes. Stir in the poultry seasoning, turn off the heat, and reserve until the broth is done.

Skim the fat from the top of the broth, and strain it into the soup pot with the sautéed vegetables; bring to a boil. Turn down to low and simmer until the vegetables are tender. Taste, and add salt and fresh ground black pepper to taste. Turn heat up to high, add the egg noodles and boil for 7 minutes. Dice the chicken and add to the pot. Turn heat down to medium and simmer until the noodles are tender.

Stir in the parsley, and serve.

Corn and Clam Chowder

This recipe is the perfect solution to the problem of not being able to decide between corn and clam chowder – hey, make both!

1 lb 10 oz clams, or 10 oz canned clams
2 tbsps dry white wine (if using fresh clams)
4 tsps butter
1 large onion, finely chopped
1 small carrot, finely diced
3 tbsps all-purpose flour
1¼ cups fish stock
¾ cup water (if using canned clams)
1 lb potatoes, diced
1 cup corn, thawed if frozen
2 cups whole milk
Salt and pepper
Chopped fresh parsley, to garnish

If using fresh clams, wash under cold running water. Discard any with broken shells or any that refuse to close when tapped. Put the clams into a heavy-bottom saucepan with the wine. Cover tightly, set over medium-high heat, and cook for 2 to 4 minutes, or until they open, shaking the pan occasionally. Discard any that remain closed. Remove the clams from the shells and strain the cooking liquid through a very fine mesh sieve; reserve both. If using canned clams, drain and rinse well.

Melt the butter in a large saucepan over medium-low heat. Add the onion and carrot and cook for 3 to 4 minutes, stirring frequently, until the onion is softened. Stir in the flour and continue cooking for 2 minutes.

Slowly add about half the stock and stir well, scraping the bottom of the pan to mix in the flour. Pour in the remaining stock and the reserved clam cooking liquid, or the water if using canned clams, and bring just to a boil, stirring.

Add the potatoes, corn, and milk and stir to combine. Reduce the heat and simmer gently, partially covered, for about 20 minutes, stirring occasionally, until all the vegetables are tender.

Chop the clams, if large. Stir in the clams and continue cooking for about 5 minutes until heated through. Taste and adjust the seasoning, if needed

Ladle the soup into bowls and sprinkle with parsley.

Cream of Broccoli Soup
with Cheddar Crouton

If we have to bribe you with cheesy cheddar croutons to get you to eat this delicious and nutritious broccoli soup, we'll do it.

2 tbsps unsalted butter
1 onion, diced
2 clove garlic, minced
2½ lbs broccoli crowns
1 quart chicken or vegetable broth
2 cups water
½ cup cream, optional
Salt and fresh ground black pepper to taste
6 slices baguette or other bread
½ cup shredded sharp cheddar cheese

In a soup pot, melt the butter over medium heat; when it begins to foam add the onion and large pinch of salt. Cook, stirring occasionally, until the onions are soft and translucent, about 10 minutes. Add the garlic and cook for another minute.

While the onions are cooking, cut the tops (florettes) off the broccoli, and set aside. Cut the stems into ¼ inch slices, add to the tops and reserve. When the onions are ready, add the broth, water, and broccoli. Bring to a simmer, and cook until the broccoli is fork-tender.

While the soup is cooking, toast the bread and place on a foil-covered sheet pan. Top with the cheese (be sure to cover entire surface so the bread doesn't burn). Place under a broiler until the cheese is melted and bubbling.

When the broccoli is ready, remove from heat and puree using a stick blender, or carefully process the soup (in small batches!) in a blender until very smooth. To be safe, place a kitchen towel over the blender, and pulse on and off to begin.

Pour back into the pot. Add the cream, if using, and cook on medium-low until heated through. Season with salt and fresh ground black pepper to taste.

Ladle the broccoli soup into bowls and top with cheese croutons.

Lobster Bisque

A freshly steamed lobster is a wonderful thing, but to taste the true essence of lobster, bisque is the way to go.

1 lb cooked lobster
3 tbsps butter
1 small carrot, grated
1 celery stalk, finely chopped
1 leek, finely chopped
1 small onion, finely chopped
2 shallots, finely chopped
3 tbsps brandy or Cognac
¼ cup dry white wine
5 cups water
1 tbsp tomato paste
½ cup heavy cream, or to taste
6 tbsps all-purpose flour
2 to 3 tbsps water
Salt and pepper
Snipped fresh chives, to garnish

Pull off the lobster tail. With the legs up, cut the body in half lengthwise. Scoop out the tomalley (the soft pale greenish-gray part) and, if it is a female, the roe (the solid red-orange part). Reserve these together, covered and refrigerated. Remove the meat and cut into bite-sized pieces; cover and refrigerate. Chop the shell into large pieces.

Melt half the butter in a large saucepan over medium heat and add the lobster shell pieces. Cook until brown bits begin to stick on the bottom of the pan. Add the carrot, celery, leek, onion, and shallots. Cook, stirring, for 1½ to 2 minutes (do not let it burn). Add the brandy and wine and bubble for 1 minute. Pour over the water, add the tomato paste and a large pinch of salt, and bring to a boil. Reduce the heat, simmer for 30 minutes, and strain the stock, discarding the solids.

Melt the remaining butter in a small saucepan and add the tomalley and roe, if any. Add the cream, whisk to mix well, remove from the heat, and set aside.

Put the flour in a small mixing bowl and very slowly whisk in the cold water. Stir in a little of the hot stock mixture to make a smooth liquid.

Bring the remaining lobster stock to a boil and whisk in the flour mixture. Boil gently for 4 to 5 minutes until the soup thickens, stirring frequently. Press the tomalley, roe, and cream mixture through a sieve into the soup. Reduce the heat and add the reserved lobster meat. Simmer gently until heated through.

Taste the soup and adjust the seasoning, adding more cream if desired. Ladle into warmed bowls, sprinkle with chives, and serve.

Serves 4

Hearty Beef Stew

Not only is this classic stew delicious, it's also a frugal dish, since it uses relatively inexpensive chuck roast. Be sure to brown the beef very well to achieve a deep, rich flavor.

3 lbs boneless chuck roast,
cut into 2 inch pieces
2 tbsps vegetable oil
1 tsp salt, plus more as needed
Freshly ground black pepper to taste
2 yellow onions, cut into 1 inch pieces
3 tbsps flour
3 cloves garlic, minced
4 cups cold beef stock or broth
3 carrots, peeled, cut into 1-inch pieces
2 stalks celery, cut into 1-inch pieces
1 tbsp ketchup
1 bay leaf
¼ tsp dried rosemary
¼ tsp dried thyme
2 lbs Yukon gold potatoes, peeled,
cut into large chunks
Fresh parsley to garnish, optional

Season the beef very generously with salt and freshly ground black pepper. Add vegetable oil to a large heavy pot or Dutch oven (one that has a tight fitting lid), and set over high heat. When the oil begins to smoke slightly, add the beef and brown very well. Work in batches if necessary. Once well-browned, remove the beef to a bowl with a slotted spoon, leaving the oil and beef drippings in the pot.

Lower the heat to medium, and add the onions to the pot; sauté about 5 minutes, or until translucent. Add the flour and cook for 2 minutes, stirring often. Add the garlic and cook for 1 minute. Whisk in 1 cup of the beef stock to deglaze the bottom of the pot, scraping up any browned bits caramelized on the bottom. Add the rest of the broth, carrots, celery, ketchup, bay leaf, thyme, rosemary, beef, and 1 tsp of salt.

Bring back to a gentle simmer, cover, and cook on low for 1 hour. Add potatoes, and simmer covered for another 30 minutes. Remove the cover, turn up the heat to medium, and cook, stirring occasionally, for another 30 minutes, or until the meat and vegetables are tender.

This last 30 minutes uncovered is not only to finish the cooking, but also to reduce and thicken the sauce. If the stew gets too thick, adjust with some more stock or water. Turn off heat, taste and adjust seasoning, and let sit for 15 minutes before serving. Garnish with fresh parsley if desired.

Serves 6

"Chili Verde" Green Pork Stew

Tomatillo-based green salsas are readily available in today's grocery stores, and make a great base for this flavorful, spicy pork stew.

2 tbsps vegetable oil
4 lbs boneless pork shoulder,
cut into 2 inch cubes
Salt and pepper to taste
1 yellow onion, chopped
2 Anaheim chilies, seeded, diced
4 cups (two 16 oz jars) green salsa (look for
one with tomatillos as the main ingredient)
2 tsps ground cumin
1 tsp dried oregano
1 tsp sugar
½ tsp chipotle pepper
Sour cream and chopped cilantro
to garnish, optional

Season the pork cubes with salt and pepper. In a heavy Dutch oven, heat the oil on medium-high, and sear the pork in batches until very well browned. Reserve the cooked pork in a bowl. Reduce the heat to medium and add the onions. Sauté until golden, about 5 minutes.

Add the rest of the ingredients, bring to a boil, reduce heat to low, cover, and simmer gently for 1½ to 2 hours, stirring occasionally, or until the pork is very tender. Taste and adjust seasoning.

Serve in bowls topped with sour cream and cilantro.

Chicken and Sausage Gumbo

This hearty Cajun/Creole stew's name is derived from the African word for okra. This signature ingredient not only gives the gumbo a great flavor, but also thickens the dish. The other key element is the "roux," which is a slowly browned mixture of flour and oil. The darker you cook the roux, the stronger the flavor.

⅓ cup vegetable oil
⅓ cup flour
1 onion, diced
3 ribs celery, large dice
2 green bell pepper, seeded, diced
½ cup minced green onions
3 cloves garlic, crushed fine
1 lb Andouille sausage, or other spicy, smoked
sausage, cut in 1 inch pieces
6 cups chicken broth
1 can (10 oz) diced tomatoes
with green chilies
1½ lbs boneless, skinless chicken thighs,
cut in 2 inch pieces
1 tbsp Cajun seasoning
1 tsp salt
¼ tsp cayenne pepper, or to taste
½ tsp black pepper
2 cups frozen cut okra, thawed, drained
1 lb shrimp, peeled, deveined
cooked white long grain rice, optional

To make the roux: In a heavy Dutch oven or pot, cook the oil and flour over medium low heat, stirring with a wooden spoon, until it's a light, nutty brown color.

Add the onion, celery, and bell pepper to the roux and cook for another 5 minutes to soften the vegetables. Add the green onions, garlic, and sausage; stir, and cook for 3 minutes.

Add the broth, tomatoes, chicken, Cajun seasoning, salt, cayenne pepper, and black pepper. Bring to a boil, reduce to low, and simmer, stirring occasionally, for 1 hour. Stir in the okra and simmer for another 30 minutes, or until the chicken is very tender.

Stir in the shrimp and cook for 3 to 4 minutes, or until they're cooked through. Taste for salt and spice, and adjust seasoning if needed. Serve hot with some cooked rice.

Serves 6

Jambalaya

This Louisiana classic is truly one of America's greatest culinary achievements. Spicy Creole jambalaya is rustic and refined all at the same time, and is legendary for its big flavored, crowd-pleasing abilities.

1 tbsp vegetable oil
1½ lbs Andouille sausage, or other spicy smoked sausage, cut in ½ inch cubes
1 lb skinless, boneless chicken thighs, cut into 1 inch pieces
1 large yellow onion, diced
1 cup diced celery
1 cup diced green bell pepper
2 tsps Cajun seasoning
1 tsp dried thyme
1 tsp salt
¼ tsp freshly ground black pepper
¼ tsp ground cayenne pepper, or to taste
2 cups uncooked long-grain rice
1 (14.5 oz) can diced tomatoes
4 cups chicken broth
1 bay leaf
1 lb shrimp, peeled, deveined
½ bunch green onions, thinly sliced
Louisiana hot sauce, optional

Heat the vegetable oil in a large Dutch oven, or other heavy pot, over medium-high heat. Add the sausage to the pan, and cook until lightly browned. Add the chicken, onion, celery, bell pepper, Cajun seasoning, salt, thyme, salt, black pepper, and cayenne. Cook for about 5 minutes, or until the onions begin to soften.

Turn up the heat to high. Add the tomatoes, broth, and bay leaf, and bring to a boil. Add the rice, and stir until completely combined. Cover, reduce heat to low, and simmer for 18 minutes. Stir in shrimp and green onions, cover, and cook 3 to 5 minutes, or until the rice is as tender as you like. Serve with hot sauce.

Note: You can really adjust this so many different ways. If you want a thinner, soupier stew add a couple extra cups of broth. If you like your rice a bit firmer, cut the cooking time a few minutes. If you like it soft (which I do), give it a couple more minutes. You can use any types of sausage, as well as things like bacon, ham, and pork shoulder. This is a fun dish to experiment with. No two Jambalayas should be alike.

Firehouse Chili con Carne

*Is this called firehouse chili because it's the kind of hearty dish firemen love,
or because of its spicy seasoning? Trick question; it's both!*

1 tbsp vegetable oil
1 large yellow onion, diced
2½ lbs lean ground beef
3 cloves garlic, minced
¼ cup chile powder
1 tbsp ground cumin
1 tsp freshly ground black pepper
½ tsp chipotle pepper
¼ tsp cayenne pepper
1 tsp dried oregano
1 tsp sugar
1 large green bell pepper, seeded and diced
1 large red bell pepper, seeded and diced
1 (15 oz) can tomato sauce
2 tbsps tomato paste
3 cups water, or more as needed
1 (15 oz) can pinto beans, drained, not rinsed
1 (15 oz) can kidney beans, drained, not rinsed

Optional garnishes...
Sour cream, grated pepper jack, diced onions,
and fresh cilantro leaves

Add the vegetable oil and onions to a Dutch oven, or other heavy pot. Place over medium-high heat and sauté for about 5 minutes, or until the onions begin to soften. Add the ground beef, and cook for about 10 minutes. As the beef browns, use a wooden spoon to break the meat into very small pieces.

Add the garlic, chili powder, ground cumin, black pepper, chipotle, cayenne, oregano, and sugar. Cook, stirring, for 2 minutes.

Stir in the bell peppers, tomato sauce, tomato paste, and water. Bring up to a simmer; reduce the heat to medium-low and cook, uncovered, stirring occasionally for 60 minutes.

After 60 minutes, stir in the beans and simmer for another 30 minutes. If needed, add more water anytime during the cooking to adjust desired thickness. Taste for salt and pepper, and adjust. Serve hot, garnished with sour cream, grated pepper jack, and fresh cilantro leaves.

Serves 6

Texas Lone Star Chili

Sometimes simply called a "bowl of red", Texas style chili has two major differences with regular chili; it uses cubed beef instead of ground, and it doesn't contain beans. Other than that, like most American recipes, anything goes!

2 tbsps vegetable oil
3 lbs boneless beef chuck,
cut in ½ inch cubes
2 green poblano chilies, seeded, diced
2 red Fresno chilies, seeded, minced
1 large onion, diced
3 cloves garlic, minced
2 tbsps ancho chili powder, or to taste
1 tbsp ground cumin
1 tsp dried oregano
1½ tsps salt
½ tsp ground black pepper
¼ tsp chipotle
¼ tsp cayenne
3 cups beef broth
1 can (10 oz) diced tomatoes
with green chilies
1 tbsp corn meal
Water as needed
¼ cup diced white onion and fresh
chopped cilantro, optional

In a Dutch oven, or cast iron pot, sear the beef in the oil over high heat, until well-browned. Do in batches if necessary. Add onions to the pot and sauté on medium heat for 5 minutes. Add the garlic and cook for one minute.

Add all remaining ingredients, except the corn meal, and bring to a boil, reduce the heat to low, cover, and simmer 1 hour, stirring occasionally. Uncover and stir in the corn meal. Continue cooking uncovered, stirring occasionally, for another hour, or until the meat is very tender. Water can be added any time during the cooking to adjust thickness. Be sure to occasionally skim off any fat that floats to the surface.

Taste for seasoning, and adjust if necessary. Serve hot garnished with white onions, cilantro, and/or any of your favorite chili fixings.

Chicken & White Bean Chili

When you're in the mood for the big, bold flavors of chili, but want something a little lighter, give this hearty version a try.

2 lbs boneless, skinless chicken thigh,
cut into 1 inch pieces
2 tbsps vegetable oil
1 onion, diced
3 cloves garlic, minced
1 tsp salt
2 tbsps ground cumin
½ tsp ground chipotle pepper
¼ tsp cinnamon
½ tsp fresh ground black pepper
1 red bell pepper, seeded, diced
1 green bell pepper, seeded, diced
1 jalapeno pepper, seeded, diced
1 can (10 oz) diced tomato with green chilies
3 cups chicken broth, more as needed
2 (15 oz) cans white kidney beans, great
northern, or navy beans, drained
Cayenne pepper to taste
Chopped fresh cilantro to garnish, optional

Add oil to a large, heavy pot over medium-high heat. When the oil's hot, add the chunks of chicken, and sauté for 5 minutes. Add the onions, garlic, and salt; cook, stirring, for another 2 minutes. Add the cumin, chipotle, cinnamon, salt, and fresh ground black pepper; cook, stirring, for another minute.

Add the red bell pepper, green bell pepper, jalapeno pepper, diced tomato with green chilies, and chicken broth. Bring to a simmer, turn heat to low, and cook, stirring occasionally, for 30 minutes.

Stir in the beans and simmer another 30 minutes. Taste and adjust for salt and pepper. Serve hot with a shake of cayenne, and cilantro if desired.

Asparagus with Lemon Butter Sauce

It's not really Spring until you see bright green plates of asparagus on the table.

2 lbs asparagus spears, trimmed
1 tbsp olive oil
Salt and pepper

For the sauce...
Juice of 1 lemon
2 tbsps water
1 stick butter cut into cubes

Pre-heat oven to 400°F.

Lay the asparagus spears out in a single layer on a large baking sheet. Drizzle over the oil, season to taste with salt and pepper and roast in the pre-heated oven for 10 minutes, or until just tender.

Meanwhile, make the sauce. Pour the lemon juice into a saucepan and add the water. Heat for a minute or so, then slowly add the butter, cube by cube, stirring constantly until it has all been incorporated.

Season to taste with pepper and serve immediately, drizzled over the asparagus.

SIDE DISHES • ASPARAGUS WITH LEMON BUTTER SAUCE

Roasted Vegetables

Roasting in a very hot oven really brings out the natural sweetness in vegetables, and intensifies their flavor.

¼ cup olive oil
1 garlic clove, peeled, left whole,
but crushed slightly
2 large red bell peppers, seeded,
cut into ½ inch strips
4 green zucchini, halved, then cut
lengthwise into quarters
1 red onion, peeled, cut in eighths
2 lbs Yukon gold potatoes, cut in wedges
4 carrots, peeled, cut in thirds,
then into ½ inch sticks
½ lemon, juiced
1 tsp fresh rosemary spring, leaves picked
2 tbsps fresh chopped parsley
Salt and fresh ground black pepper to taste

Pre-heat oven to 450°F.

In a small saucepan, warm the oil and garlic over low heat, until the garlic begins to bubble. Turn off the heat and allow to sit for 30 minutes to infuse the oil. Remove the garlic clove and reserve the oil.

Add the remaining ingredients to a large mixing bowl, along with the garlic oil. Toss to coat completely.

Arrange in a single layer on one or more foil lined baking sheets. Roast for 20 minutes in pre-heated oven. Remove and stir the vegetables so they cook evenly. Put back in and roast for another 25 to 35 minutes, or until the vegetable are tender and the edges are browned.

Season with additional salt and fresh ground black pepper to taste. Serve hot, sprinkled with freshly chopped parsley.

Serves 6-8

Creamy Corn Custard

This corn custard recipe is light, but still rich and satisfying. Since it's so soft and creamy, texturally, it makes a great match for things like barbecue pork ribs, grilled steaks, and fried fish.

3 cups corn kernels, fresh, or thawed frozen
1½ cups heavy cream
½ cup milk
1¼ tsp salt
Pinch of cayenne
3 egg yolks
4 eggs
Butter as needed
8 (6 oz) oven-proof ramekins, buttered

Pre-heat oven to 325°F.

Add the corn, cream, milk, salt, and cayenne to a saucepan. Bring to a simmer over medium heat. Turn off heat and remove to cool slightly. Carefully pour into a blender and puree until very smooth. Reserve.

Add the eggs and egg yolks to a mixing bowl and whisk for 30 seconds. Slowly, a cup at a time, stir in the warm corn custard mixture. When everything is combined, ladle the mixture into 8 well buttered, 6 oz ramekins.

Fill a roasting pan or casserole dish with 1-inch of hot water and place in the filled ramekins. Bake for 35 minutes, or until the corn custard is just set. Remove from the baking dish and let cool for 15 minutes before serving.

May be eaten out of the ramekins – or run a parry knife around the inside, and turn over on to a plate for a "fancier" presentation.

SIDE DISHES • CREAMY CORN CUSTARD

Braised Red Cabbage & Apples

Red cabbage absorbs new flavors extremely well, and the addition of the vinegar makes this a delicious side dish.

1 tsp of whole caraway seeds
1 tbsp vegetable oil
1 red onion, halved and thinly sliced
2 tbsps brown sugar
1 small red cabbage, shredded
2 apples, peeled and thinly sliced
2 tbsps red wine
½ cup apple juice
2 tbsps cider vinegar
Salt and freshly ground black pepper
1 tsp lemon juice

In a saucepan over medium heat, dry roast the caraway seeds for about 1 minute until they start to give off an aroma.

Heat the oil in a large pot over medium heat, add the onion, and sauté for 5 minutes until it becomes translucent. Add the brown sugar, stir, and add the cabbage and apples. Stir for a few minutes until the cabbage wilts. Add in the red wine, apple juice, and vinegar. Add the toasted caraway seeds and salt and pepper to taste. Bring the mixture to a boil, lower to a simmer, add the lemon juice, cover, and cook for 30 minutes.

Note: Braised cabbage is wonderful served with chicken, meat, or pork dishes.

Succulent Succotash

This is a modern take on a very old Native American staple, and makes a great, colorful side dish for almost any meal.

1 tbsp olive oil
½ tbsp butter
½ yellow onion, diced
3 garlic cloves, minced
1 jalapeno or other small hot chile pepper, sliced
½ red bell pepper, diced
½ cup diced tomatoes, fresh if available
4 oz green beans, cut in ½ inch pieces
1½ cups fresh or frozen corn
1 cup frozen baby lima beans, thawed
1 cup cubed green zucchini
½ tsp ground cumin
Pinch of cayenne
¼ cup water
Salt and freshly ground black pepper to taste

Place a large skillet on medium heat, and add the olive oil and butter. When the butter foams up, add the onions and a big pinch of salt. Sauté for about 5 minutes, or until the onions begin to soften and turn golden.

Add the garlic, jalapeno, and bell pepper; sauté for 3 minutes. Add the rest of the ingredients, and cook, stirring occasionally until the vegetables are tender. More liquid may be added if the mixture gets too dry. When done, taste for salt, and adjust the seasoning if needed. Serve immediately.

Green Bean Casserole

This rich, decadent green bean casserole is strictly for those special occasions meals where counting calories is not even a remote consideration.

1½ lbs green beans, trimmed, cut in thirds
1½ cups cream
½ cup chicken broth
1 clove garlic, minced fine
½ tsp salt
¼ tsp freshly ground black pepper
Pinch of nutmeg
1 (6 oz) can French fried onions, divided

Pre-heat oven to 375°F.

Bring a pot of well-salted water to boil. Blanch the beans in the boiling water for 5 minutes. Drain very well and reserve.

Add the cream, broth, garlic, salt, and nutmeg to a small saucepan. Place over medium heat and cook, stirring occasionally, until the mixture comes to a simmer. Remove from heat and reserve.

Spread half the French fried onions in the bottom of a 2 quart casserole dish. Spread the beans evenly over the onions. Pour over the cream mixture. Use a fork to press the beans down into the cream. Top with the other half of the fried onions. Use a fork to flatten the top, pressing down firmly.

Bake for 25 to 30 minutes, or until the beans are very tender, and the casserole is browned and bubbling. Remove and let rest for 15 minutes before serving.

Steakhouse Creamed Spinach

This is the king of the steakhouse side dishes. It's not a real steak dinner unless there's creamed spinach on the table.

½ cup unsalted butter
24 oz pre-washed, ready-to-use baby spinach
½ onion, finely diced
1 whole clove
3 cloves garlic, very finely minced
⅓ cup flour
1½ cups cold milk
Pinch freshly ground nutmeg
Salt and pepper, to taste

Put a large stockpot over high heat. Add 1 tbsp of the butter, and as soon as it melts, dump in all the spinach and cover quickly. Leave for one minute, uncover, and continue cooking, stirring the spinach with a long wooden spoon, until just barely wilted. Transfer to a colander to drain.

When the spinach is cool enough to handle, squeeze as much liquid out as possible, and roughly chop. Press between paper towels to draw out the last of the water, and reserve until needed.

Melt the rest of the butter in a saucepan over medium heat. Add the onions and cook for about 5 minutes, or until translucent. Whisk in the flour and cook for 3 minutes, stirring. Add the garlic and cook for 1 minute. Pour in the cold milk, whisking constantly, and cook until it comes to a simmer. Reduce heat to low and simmer for another 5 minutes. The sauce will thicken as it cooks.

Season the sauce with nutmeg, salt and fresh ground black pepper to taste. Add the spinach, and stir to combine. The dish is ready to serve as soon as the spinach is heated through. Taste once more, and adjust seasoning before serving.

Serves 4-6

Roasted Artichokes

Artichokes are so naturally delicious, and this simple roasting technique concentrates the flavors even more.

6 whole large artichokes
3 lemons, halved
6 cloves garlic, peeled, left whole
6 tbsps olive oil
Salt to taste

Using a serrated knife, cut off the stem of the artichoke where it meets the base. Turn the artichoke around and cut off 1 inch of the top. Quickly rub each artichoke with a cut lemon so they don't discolor.

Tear off 4 square pieces of foil. Rub a few drops of olive oil on the foil and place an artichoke stem side down. Use your fingers to loosen the leaves in the center. Stick a clove of garlic into the center and push down an inch or so. Sprinkle over a large pinch of salt. Drizzle 1 tbsp olive oil over the top. Finish by squeezing the half lemon over the top. The lemon juice will "wash" the salt and olive down in between the leaves.

Gather up the corners of the foil and press together on top to tightly seal the artichoke (like a chocolate kiss). Wrap in a second piece of foil to form a tight seal.

Repeat with the other artichokes. Place in a roasting pan and bake at 425°F. for 1 hour and 15 minutes. Let rest for 15 minutes before unwrapping and serving.

Can be eaten hot, warm, or chilled.

Serves 6

Boston Baked Beans

They don't call Boston "Beantown" for nothing. This great American side dish has been spreading happiness at picnics and potlucks for hundreds of years.

1 pound dry navy beans
6 cups water
pinch of baking soda
1 bay leaf
6 strips bacon, cut in 1/2-inch pieces
(traditionally salt pork is used, and if desired 4 ounces can be substituted for the bacon)
1 yellow onion, diced
⅓ cup molasses
¼ cup packed dark brown sugar
1 teaspoon dry mustard
1½ teaspoon salt, or to taste
½ teaspoon freshly ground black pepper

Pre-heat oven to 300°F.

Soak the beans in the 6 cups of water overnight in a large saucepan or Dutch oven. Add a pinch of baking soda and bay leaf, and bring to a boil. Reduce the heat to medium and simmer for 10 minutes. Drain into a colander set over a large bowl, and reserve the liquid.

Transfer the drained beans into a small Dutch oven, or a 2 1/2-quart bean pot if you have one, and add the rest of the ingredients. Stir until combined. Add enough of the reserved water to just barely cover the beans.

Cover the pot tightly and place in the oven for 1 hour. Uncover and check the liquid level. Add some more reserved liquid if the beans are getting too dry. Cover and cook 1 more hour. Uncover and test the beans; they should be starting to get tender, but if they're still firm, cover and cook a bit longer, adding a splash of water if they're getting too dry.

When just tender, turn the heat up to 350 degrees F., and continue to cook uncovered for another 30 minutes or so. This last 30 minutes is to reduce the liquid a bit, to create a thick, syrupy consistency. Remove when ready, and serve hot or room temperature.

Note: The cooking times will vary based on the size and shape of the baking vessel, but the process will not. Simply bake the beans covered until just tender, and finish uncovered until the liquid has thickened slightly.

Serves 10

Classic Cole Slaw

This very simple cole slaw is a great all-purpose recipe for any picnic or barbecue.

2 lbs thinly sliced green cabbage
2 carrots, peeled, grated or finely julienned
on a vegetable slicer
½ cup pineapple juice
1 cup mayonnaise
2 tsps sugar
¼ tsp cayenne pepper, or to taste
Salt and fresh ground black pepper to taste

Place the cabbage and carrot in a large mixing bowl. In a smaller bowl, whisk together the rest of the ingredients. Taste and adjust the sweetness and spiciness if so desired. Pour over the cabbage mixture and toss until coated.

Best if dressed within 30 minutes of serving, so it stays crisp and fresh.

Taste for seasoning and toss again right before serving.

Makes 12 portions

Macaroni & Cheese

Did you know that Thomas Jefferson is credited with inventing macaroni and cheese? That has nothing to do with the recipe, but it's good to know in case you end up on one of those trivia game shows.

6 tbsps butter, divided
½ cup minced onion
3 tbsps all-purpose flour
2¾ cups milk
½ tsp freshly chopped thyme leaves
(or pinch of dry), optional
Small pinch of nutmeg
Pinch of cayenne
Salt and pepper to taste
2 heaping cups dry elbow macaroni
½ lb shredded cheddar cheese
¼ lb shredded Gruyere cheese,
or other high-quality Swiss cheese
⅔ cup breadcrumbs

Pre-heat oven to 350°F.

Melt 4 tbsps of the butter in a medium saucepan over medium heat. Sauté the onions in the butter for 4 to 5 minutes, until translucent. Do not brown. Stir in the flour, and cook for 2 minutes. Whisk in the cold milk, and cook, stirring, until the mixture comes to a simmer and thickens slightly. Turn off the heat and stir in the thyme, nutmeg, pinch of cayenne, salt and pepper to taste. Set aside until needed.

Boil the elbow macaroni in salted water, one minute less than the package directions state. Drain well and add to a large mixing bowl. Add the white sauce, and the cheeses, and fold with a spatula until thoroughly combined.

Transfer into a lightly buttered 9 x 13 inch baking dish. Melt 2 tbsps of butter and mix with the breadcrumbs. Scatter evenly over the top of the casserole. Bake for 40 to 45 minutes, or until bubbly and golden brown.

Note: Cover loosely with foil towards the end of the cooking, if the top is getting too brown for your liking.

Glazed Yams

A simple lemon and brown sugar glaze is all that's needed to bring out the yam's natural earthy sweetness.

1 lemon, juiced
2½ lbs Garnet, or other orange-fleshed yams
2 tbsps unsalted butter
¼ cup packed brown sugar
½ tsp salt, or to taste
⅛ tsp cayenne

Pre-heat oven to 350°F.

Add the lemon juice to a large mixing bowl. Peel yams, cut in 1 inch cubes, and toss with the lemon juice.

Melt the butter in a large skillet over medium-high heat. Add the yams and lemon juice, brown sugar, salt, and cayenne. Cook, stirring, for about 5 to 7 minutes, until a sticky syrup is formed and the edges of the yams begin to caramelize.

Remove from heat and transfer into a lightly buttered, oven-proof baking dish. Bake for 20 to 25 minutes or until tender. Serve hot.

Serves 6-8

Perfect Mashed Potatoes

Almost everyone loves smooth, creamy mashed potato. But it has to be smooth and creamy, not lumpy. A potato masher is invaluable but I prefer a potato ricer, which presses the potato through tiny holes and makes fine 'worms' which means you never get lumps.

2 lbs of potatoes, such as Russet potatoes
2 oz butter
3 tbsps milk
Salt and pepper

Peel the potatoes, placing them in cold water as you prepare the others to prevent them from going brown.

Cut the potatoes into even-sized chunks and cook in a large saucepan of boiling salted water over a medium heat, covered, for 20 to 25 minutes until they are tender. Test with the point of a knife, but do make sure you test right to the middle to avoid lumps.

Remove the pan from the heat and drain the potatoes. Return the potatoes to the hot pan and mash with a potato masher until smooth.

Add the butter and continue to mash until it is all mixed in, then add the milk.

Taste the mash and season with salt and pepper as necessary. Serve at once.

Variations: For herb mash, mix in 3 tbsps chopped fresh parsley, thyme or mint. For mustard or horseradish mash, mix in 2 tbsps wholegrain mustard or horseradish sauce. For pesto mash, stir in 4 tbsps fresh pesto and for nutmeg mash, grate ½ a nutmeg into the mash and add 125 ml/4 fl oz natural yogurt. To make creamed potato, add 125 ml/4 fl oz soured cream and 2 tbsps snipped fresh chives.

Serves 4

Baked Acorn Squash

These buttery, caramelized beauties sure would look nice on a table next to large, roasted pieces of meat.

2 acorn squash
2 tbsps freshly squeezed orange juice
1 tbsp brown sugar
2 tbsps unsalted butter
2 tbsps real maple syrup
Salt and fresh ground black pepper to taste

Pre-heat oven to 400°F.

Cut the acorn squash in half lengthwise, and scoop the seeds and strings out of the cavity. Carefully score the inside of each squash with a sharp knife, making ⅛ inch deep cuts about ½ inch apart (refer to mouthwatering photo). Use a brush to paint each half with the orange juice. Sprinkle generously with salt. Bake for 30 minutes.

In a small saucepan, combine the brown sugar, butter, maple syrup and fresh ground black pepper. Bring to a boil, stir, and cook for one minute. Reserve.

Remove the squash from the oven, and spoon off any liquid that has accumulated in the cavities. Brush the glaze evenly over each, and bake for another 40 minutes, or until tender and caramelized on the edges. Allow to sit for 15 minutes before serving, possibly with a bit more salt sprinkled over.

For an extra nice glaze, baste squash with the syrup that collects in the cavity a few times while it's baking.

Cheesy Broccoli Gratin

You'll forget all about how nutritious fresh broccoli is when you see this crispy, bubbling, golden-brown beauty coming to the table.

¼ cup butter
¼ cup flour
2 cups cold milk
Pinch of nutmeg
Pinch of cayenne
1 tsp fresh thyme leaves, chopped (optional)
8 oz extra-sharp cheddar cheese, shredded
½ tsp salt, or to taste
2 lbs fresh broccoli crowns, cut into
2 inch pieces
½ cup plain breadcrumbs
2 tbsps melted butter
2 tbsps grated Parmesan cheese

Pre-heat oven to 375°F.

Melt the butter in a saucepan over medium heat, and add the flour. Cook, stirring, for about 3 minutes (the mixture should begin to smell like cooked piecrust). Slowly whisk in the cold milk. Continue whisking until there are no visible lumps. Add the nutmeg, cayenne, and thyme. The sauce will thicken as it comes back to a simmer. Reduce the heat to low, and simmer, stirring occasionally, for 10 minutes.

Turn off the heat, and stir in the cheese. When all the cheese has melted into the sauce, season with salt, and reserve until needed.

Note: Sauce may be strained if you are concerned about lumps.

Bring a pot of salted water to a rapid boil. Add the broccoli and cook for about 5 minutes, or just until the stem ends begin to get tender. Do not overcook, as the broccoli will cook further in the oven. Drain very well (otherwise the gratin will be watery). Transfer to a large mixing bowl.

Pour over the cheese sauce, and fold with a spatula until the broccoli is completely coated with the sauce. Transfer into a lightly buttered 2 quart casserole dish, using the spatula to distribute evenly. In a small bowl combine breadcrumbs, butter, and Parmesan. Sprinkle evenly over the top, and oven-bake for 25 minutes, or until the top is browned and bubbly.

Scalloped Potatoes

For those times when regular potatoes just won't do. This creamy, cheesy scoop of side dish heaven looks great next to any meaty main course.

2 tbsps butter, divided
1 tbsp all-purpose flour
1 cup cream
2 cups milk
1 tsp salt
Pinch of nutmeg
Pinch of white pepper
4 springs fresh thyme
2 cloves garlic minced
4½ lbs russet potatoes, sliced thin
Salt and freshly ground black pepper to taste
4 oz grated Swiss gruyere or white cheddar

Pre-heat oven to 375°F.

Use half the butter to grease a 15 x 10 inch baking dish.

Melt the rest of the butter in a saucepan over medium heat. Whisk in the flour, and cook, stirring constantly, for 2 minutes. Whisk in the cream and milk, and bring to a simmer. Add the salt, nutmeg, white pepper, thyme, and garlic. Reduce heat to low, and simmer for 5 minutes. Remove the thyme springs; reserve.

Layer half the potatoes in the baking dish. Season generously with salt and freshly ground black pepper. Top with half of the milk mixture. Top with half the cheese. Repeat with the remaining potatoes, sauce, and cheese.

Bake for about 1 hour, or until the top is browned and the potatoes are tender. Let rest for 15 minutes before serving.

Garlic & Herb Steak Fries

Unless you have a commercial deep fryer in your kitchen, regular French fries are probably best left to the neighborhood burger joint. On the contrary, these crusty and delicious, oven-roasted steak fries are easily made at home.

4 medium russet potatoes, scrubbed and rinsed
3 tbsps olive oil
4 cloves garlic, minced and mashed against
the cutting board with the flat of a knife
½ tsp dried rosemary, crushed fine
½ tsp dried oregano
½ tsp dried thyme
½ tsp paprika
½ tsp freshly ground black pepper
1 tsp salt

Pre-heat oven to 425°F.

Cut each potato in half lengthwise. Cut each half, lengthwise, into 4 equally sized wedges. Add the potato wedges to a large mixing bowl with the rest of the ingredients. Toss meticulously to coat the potatoes evenly.

Line a sheet pan with foil. Place the potato wedges, skin side down, on the foil. Be sure to space evenly, so they cook uniformly.

Bake for 35 to 40 minutes, or until well-browned, crusty-edged, and tender. Serve immediately, sprinkled with more salt if desired.

Crispy Onion Rings

Japanese breadcrumbs, called Panko, are available in most large supermarkets, and when combined with this simple batter, produces onion rings so crispy, they defy the laws of nature.

½ cup all-purpose flour
¼ cup cornstarch
2 tablespoons instant mashed potatoes
big pinch of cayenne
1 cup cold club soda
2-3 cups panko (Japanese-style breadcrumbs), or as needed
fine salt to taste
vegetable oil for frying
2-3 yellow onions, cut into ¼-inch rings

Sift together the flour and cornstarch. Add the instant mashed potatoes, cayenne and club soda. Whisk to combine. Let sit in the fridge for 10 minutes. Meanwhile, heat vegetable oil to 350 degrees F. Pour the breadcrumbs into a shallow dish.

Remove batter from the fridge and check for consistency. The mixture should resemble a slightly thick pancake batter. More club soda can be added to adjust. Working in batches, use a fork to coat the onion rings in the batter, let the excess drip off, and then toss in the panko to coat on both sides.

Fry for about 2-3 minutes, turning over in the oil halfway through, until crispy and golden brown. Drain on a rack, and serve warm, sprinkled with salt.

Note: Regular breadcrumbs can be used, but the panko makes for a much crispier onion ring.

Serves 8-10

Hoppin' John

It's a southern tradition to invite friends and family in for a bowl of Hoppin' John on New Year's Day. Legend maintains that the more black-eye peas you eat, the more prosperous the year will be. Whereas, without a bowl of Hoppin' John, only bad luck will follow.

1 unsmoked ham hock, weighing
2 lbs 12 oz
1 cup dried black-eye peas, soaked overnight
2 large celery stalks, broken in half
1 bay leaf
1 large onion, chopped
1 dried red chili (optional)
1 tbsp rendered bacon fat, or corn or peanut oil
1 cup long-grain rice
Salt and pepper

To serve...
Hot pepper sauce
Freshly cooked greens

Put the ham hock into a large, flameproof casserole with water to cover over high heat. Bring to a boil, skimming the surface. Cover, reduce the heat, and let simmer for 1½ hours.

Stir in the drained peas, celery, bay leaf, onion, and chili, if using, and let simmer for an additional 1½ to 2 hours, or until the peas are tender but not mushy and the ham hock feels tender when you prod it with a knife.

Strain the "pot likker" (as the cooking liquid is described in old recipes) into a large bowl and reserve. Set the ham hock aside and set the peas aside separately, removing and discarding the flavorings.

Heat the bacon fat in a pan or flameproof casserole with a tight-fitting lid over medium heat. Add the rice and stir until coated with the fat. Stir in 2 cups of the reserved cooking liquid, the peas, and salt and pepper to taste. (Use the remaining cooking liquid for soup, or discard.) Bring to a boil, stirring constantly, then reduce the heat to very low, cover, and let simmer for 20 minutes without lifting the lid.

Meanwhile, cut the meat from the ham hock, discarding the skin and excess fat. Cut the meat into bite-size pieces.

Remove the pan from the heat and let stand for 5 minutes, again without lifting the lid. Fluff up the rice and peas with a fork and stir in the ham, then pile onto a warmed serving dish. Serve with a bottle of hot pepper sauce on the side and some cooked greens and cornbread.

Braised Beef Short Ribs

This is one of those recipes that will warm you from the inside out.

3½ lbs (8 pieces) beef short ribs
Salt and fresh ground black pepper as needed
4 slices bacon, cut in ½ inch pieces
1 large onion, diced
1 rib celery, diced
4 cloves garlic, minced
2 tbsps flour
1 cup dry sherry wine
3 cups beef broth, or veal stock if available
6 springs fresh thyme
1 bay leaf
2 tsp tomato paste

Pre-heat oven to 350°F.

Add the bacon to a heavy Dutch oven and fry over a medium heat on the stove top until the fat is rendered out. Remove the bacon with a slotted spoon and reserve, leaving the fat in the pan.

Turn the stove heat up to medium-high, and brown the short ribs very well on all sides. Remove the short ribs and reserve. Add the onions and celery; reduce the heat to medium, and sauté for about 5 minutes, until the onions soften.

Add the garlic and flour; cook, stirring, for 2 minutes. Whisk in the sherry (by the way, don't even think of using cooking sherry); turn heat up to high, and bring to a boil, scraping off any browned bits. Add the beef broth, tomato paste, thyme, bay leaf, beef short ribs, and ½ tsp of salt.

When the liquid returns to a simmer, cover tightly, and place in the oven. Braise for 2 hours, or until the meat is fork tender. Skim any excess fat from the top. Taste and adjust the seasoning. Serve the short ribs with the sauce spooned over.

All-American Meatloaf

Many consider a plate of meatloaf and mashed potatoes to be the quintessential American comfort food. This modern version uses lots of aromatic vegetables to add moisture and flavor.

3 cloves garlic, peeled
½ cup diced carrot
½ cup diced celery
½ cup diced yellow onion
½ cup red bell pepper, fresh or jarred
4 large white mushrooms, sliced
1 tbsp olive oil
2 tbsps butter
1 tsp dried thyme
2 tsps finely minced fresh rosemary
1 tsp Worcestershire sauce
¼ cup ketchup
½ tsp cayenne
2½ lbs ground chuck
2 tsps salt
1 tsp black pepper
2 eggs, beaten
1 cup plain bread crumbs

For the glaze...
2 tbsps brown sugar
2 tbsps ketchup
1 tbsp Dijon mustard
Pinch of salt

Pre-heat oven to 325°F.

Add the garlic, carrot, celery, onion, red bell pepper, and white mushrooms into a food processor. Pulse on and off until the vegetables are very finely minced (several times during the processing, scrape down the sides of the bowl with a spatula so the vegetables mince evenly).

Add the butter and olive oil to a large skillet and fry over a medium heat. When the butter melts, add the vegetable mixture and cook, stirring, about 10 minutes. The vegetables are done when most of the excess moisture has evaporated, and the mixture is lightly caramelized.

Remove from the heat and stir in the thyme, rosemary, Worcestershire, ketchup, and cayenne pepper. Set aside and let cool to room temperature.

Add the ground beef (which should very cold), to a large mixing bowl. Very gently break up the meat with your fingertips. Pour in the cooled vegetable mixture, salt, black pepper, and eggs. Gently combine the mixture with your fingers for just 30 seconds. Add the breadcrumbs and continue mixing until combined. The less you work the meat, the better texture the meatloaf will have.

Lightly grease a shallow roasting pan with a few drops of olive oil. Place the meatloaf mixture in the center. Wet your hands with cold water and form into a loaf shape; about 6 inches wide, by 4 inches high. Wet your hands again and smooth the surface. Place in the center of the preheated oven and set the timer for 30 minutes.

In the meantime, whisk together the brown sugar, ketchup, Dijon, and pinch of salt in a small bowl to make the glaze. After 30 minutes, remove the meatloaf and evenly spread the glaze over the top with a spoon. Spread some glaze down the sides as well.

Return to the oven and continue baking for about 35 to 45 minutes, or until you reach an internal temperature of 155°F. Remove and let rest for at least 15 minutes before slicing and serving.

Serves 6-8

Sloppy Joes

The secret to a great Sloppy Joe sandwich is slowly simmering the beefy mixture down until it's rich and tender. By the way, you should always serve Sloppy Joes with a fork, but you should never need to use it.

1½ lbs lean ground beef
½ onion, diced
2 cloves garlic, minced
1 diced green bell pepper
2 cups water, divided
¾ cup ketchup
1½ tbsps brown sugar
1 tsp Dijon mustard
Dash of Worcestershire sauce
1½ tsps salt, or to taste
½ tsp ground black pepper
Cayenne to taste
Hamburger buns

Place the ground beef and onions into a cold, large skillet and put over medium heat. Cook, stirring, until the beef begins to brown. As it cooks, break the meat into very small pieces with a spatula. The smaller the better.

Add the garlic and green pepper; cook stirring for 2 minutes. Add 1 cup of water. Bring to a simmer, scraping the bottom of the pan with a spatula to dissolve any browned bits.

Stir in the ketchup, brown sugar, mustard, Worcestershire, salt, pepper, and last cup of water. Bring to a simmer, reduce heat to low, and simmer for 30 to 45 minutes, or until most of the liquid has been evaporated, and the meat mixture is thick, rich and tender. Taste and adjust the seasoning. Serve hot on soft rolls.

Yankee Pot Roast

This recipe uses a "7-bone" chuck roast (named for the numerical shape of the bone), which is a tough, but super-flavorful cut of beef that becomes beautifully fork-tender after a long, slow braise.

"7-bone" beef chuck roast, or any large
chuck roast (about 5 lbs)
Salt and fresh ground black pepper to taste
2 tbsps vegetable oil
1 tbsp butter
1 onion, diced
2 ribs celery, chopped
2 tbsps flour
3 cloves garlic, minced
½ cup red wine
2 tsps tomato paste
2 cups chicken broth
1 bay leaf
1 tsp dried thyme
½ tsp salt
1½ lbs new potatoes
4 carrots, peeled, cut in large chunks
1 lb parsnips, peeled, cut in large chunks
1 tbsp melted butter
2 tbsps fresh chopped parsley

Pre-heat oven to 425°F.

Generously season both sides of the beef with salt and fresh ground black pepper. Place a Dutch oven on a high heat on the stove, add the vegetable oil. When the oil is hot, brown the beef very well, about 5 minutes per side. It's important to get a nice brown crust on the meat. Remove the meat to a platter, and turn the heat down to medium.

Add the butter, diced onions, celery, and a pinch of salt. Sauté for 4 to 5 minutes to brown slightly, then add the flour. Cook, stirring, 2 minutes. Add the garlic, cook, stirring, for 1 minute. Whisk in the wine, scraping to deglaze the browned bits from the bottom of the pot. Add the tomato paste, and when the mixture begins to boil, pour in the chicken broth.

Add the bay leaf, thyme, and salt. When the liquid comes to a simmer, stir well, and place the beef back into the pot. Turn the stove heat down to very low, and simmer gently for about 45 minutes per pound, or until fork tender. After 2 hours, carefully turn the beef over, and continuing cooking until done.

While the pot roast is cooking, prepare the vegetables.

Add the potatoes, carrots, and parsnips to a shallow roasting pan. Skim a tbsp of beef fat from the surface of the beef's braising liquid. Drizzle it over the vegetables, along with the melted butter. Toss the vegetables to coat, and season with salt and fresh ground black pepper. Roast in the oven for 20 minutes, or until the vegetables are almost tender. Remove and reserve.

About 30 minutes before the beef is done, uncover and add the vegetables to the pot. Continue cooking until the beef and vegetables are tender. Skim any remaining pools of fat from the gravy. Taste and adjust for salt and pepper.

Remove the beef to a large platter. It can be cut into thick slices or simply torn into large chucks, and served along with the vegetables and gravy. Top with fresh parsley.

Chicken Fried Steak With Country Cream Gravy

You can use other cuts of beef, like round steak, for this recipe, but the nooks and crannies that the cube steak provides make it ideal for this truck stop classic. This old-fashioned milk gravy is a classic topping for chicken fried steak, but it's also amazing served over buttermilk biscuits for a very hearty breakfast.

4 (6 oz) beef cube steaks
Salt and freshly ground black pepper to taste
1 cup all-purpose flour
1 tbsp paprika
½ tsp white pepper
2 eggs, beaten
¼ cup milk
Vegetable oil as needed

For the gravy...
4 oz ground pork sausage, or pork sausage link with casing removed
3 green onions, light parts chopped, green parts sliced and reserved
3 tbsps butter
¼ cup all-purpose flour
2½ cups cold milk
Salt and freshly ground black pepper to taste
Pinch of cayenne

Season both sides of the cube steaks generously with salt and pepper.

Whisk together the eggs and milk in a pie pan and reserve. Add the flour, paprika, and white pepper into a second pie pan, and mix well to combine.

One at a time, dip the cube steaks into the egg mixture, turning to coat completely, and then dredge in the flour, coating both sides. Place the egged and floured steaks on a plate, and allow to rest for 10 minutes.

Add about a ¼ inch of vegetable oil to a large skillet, and place over medium-high heat. When the oil begins to shimmer, add the steaks and cook about 3 to 4 minutes per side, until golden brown and cooked through.

Remove and drain for a couple minutes on a wire rack set over some paper towels. If working in batches, keep the cooked steaks in a warm oven until the rest are done.

Gravy: Lightly brown the sausage in a medium saucepan over medium heat. As it cooks, break the meat up into very small pieces with a wooden spoon. Add the light parts of the green onion and the butter; sauté for a few minutes, until the onions are translucent.

Stir in the flour and cook this pasty mixture for 3 minutes. Whisk in the cold milk gradually until combined. The gravy will thicken as it comes up to a simmer. When it simmers, reduce the heat to low and cook, stirring occasionally, for 15 minutes. Before serving, season with salt, pepper, and cayenne to taste.

Note: The thickness of this gravy is easily adjusted by adding another splash of milk towards the end of the cooking process.

Serves 4

New York Strip Steak & Mushrooms

Pan-seared strip steaks with sautéed mushrooms is a classic combination. The secret to bringing out the earthy goodness is to make sure they're thoroughly browned before finishing the salad.

For the mushroom salad...
¼ cup olive oil
2 tbsps butter
2 lbs large button mushrooms, thickly sliced
3 tbsps sherry vinegar
2 garlic cloves, minced fine
1 tbsp fresh chopped tarragon
Salt and fresh ground black pepper to taste

For the steaks...
4 thick-cut (10 oz) New York strip steaks
Salt and coarse-ground black pepper to taste
1 tbsp vegetable oil
¼ cup chicken broth
1 tbsp cold butter

Melt the butter in the olive oil, in a large frying pan, over medium-high heat. When the butter starts to sizzle, add the mushrooms and cook, stirring, for 10 to 15 minutes, or until the mushroom juices have evaporated, and they're very well browned. Stir in the garlic, and cook for 2 minutes.

Pour in the vinegar, and as soon as it starts to boil, turn off the heat. Transfer into a bowl, and allow to cool to room temperature. Add the tarragon, salt, and freshly ground black pepper to taste. Reserve until needed.

Season the steaks generously on both sides with salt and coarse-ground black pepper. Place a large heavy skillet over medium-high heat. Add the oil, and when hot, sear the steaks for about 5 to 6 minutes per side for medium-rare. Remove to a plate to rest.

Turn up the heat and add the mushrooms. Add the broth and use a wooden spoon to scrape the bottom of the pan. Once the broth has deglazed the caramelized meat juices from the bottom of the pan, add the butter and stir until it disappears. Turn up the heat and add the mushrooms mix to mixture. Stir to combine. Taste and adjust seasoning.

Place the steaks on warm plates and spoon over the warm mushrooms. Serve immediately.

Serves 4

'The Best' Grilled Marinated Flank Steak

An easy overnight marinade is the secret to this delicious grilled flank steak. It's not called "the best" for nothing – get ready for some juicy, flavorful beef!

4 cloves garlic, minced
¼ cup olive oil
¼ cup brown sugar
2 tbsps red wine vinegar
¼ cup soy sauce
1 tsp Dijon mustard
1 tsp freshly ground black pepper
1 whole trimmed flank steak
(about 1½ to 2 lbs)
Salt to taste

Add all the ingredients, except the flank steak and salt, into a large, zip top freezer bag. Seal and shake to combine. Add the flank steak and reseal the bag, squeezing out most of the air. Refrigerate for at least 6 hours, but better overnight.

Remove the flank steak from the marinade to a large plate. The marinade can be poured in a small saucepan, boiled, and served with the cooked steak. Pat the flank steak dry with paper towels. Season both sides with salt and freshly ground black pepper to taste. Let sit out at room temperature for 15 minutes. Preheat your grill. Brush a little oil on the grates and place the steak on the grill.

Grill over high direct heat for 5 to 6 minutes per side for medium-rare, or until it reaches your desired degree of doneness. Transfer to a clean plate and loosely cover with foil. Let rest for 10 minutes before cutting into thin slices across the grain.

Note: This flank steak is best cooked over a hot charcoal fire, but it will also work on a gas grill, indoor grill pan, or broiler.

Serves 4-6

"London Broil" with Brown Gravy

London broil is not a cut of beef, but instead a way to prepare it. London broil is usually made with a thick top round steak, but can also be done with flank or sirloin steak. By the way, leftover London broil makes fantastic cold roast beef sandwiches.

¼ cup balsamic vinegar
2 tbsps olive oil
4 cloves crushed garlic
½ tsp dried rosemary
2 lbs top round "London Broil" steak,
about 2 inches thick
1 tbsp freshly ground black pepper
Kosher salt as needed
1 bunch green onions, washed

For the gravy...
½ cup butter
½ yellow onion, diced
½ cup all-purpose flour
1 clove garlic, minced
1 quart cold beef broth
(as high-quality as possible!)
2 tsps tomato paste
1 tsp Dijon mustard
1 tsp Worcestershire sauce
Salt and black pepper to taste

In a small bowl whisk together the vinegar, oil, garlic, and rosemary. Place the beef on a plate and poke both sides all over with a fork. Transfer to a plastic freezer bag and pour in the marinade. Squeeze out the air, seal, and refrigerate overnight.

Turn broiler on high. Make a bed of green onions on an oven-safe pan. Remove the London broil from the marinade and pat dry. Brush both sides lightly with vegetable oil. Salt and pepper generously on both sides.

Place on the pan, over the onions. Broil about 6 inches under the flame for approximately 7 to 8 minutes per side for medium rare, or to an internal temperature of 130°F.

Transfer to a plate and cover loosely with foil; let rest for 10 minutes. To serve, cut against the grain into thin slices. Serve topped with hot beef gravy.

For the gravy: In a saucepan, melt the butter over medium heat. Add the onions, cooking until they are golden brown. Add the flour and cook, stirring, for about 5 minutes, or until the mixture is golden-brown and smells like cooked piecrust.

Add the garlic and cook for 30 seconds. Whisk in the cold beef broth one cup at a time, and then add the rest of the ingredients, except the salt and pepper.

Bring to a simmer, whisking, then reduce the heat to low and simmer for 25 minutes, stirring occasionally. Taste and adjust the seasoning if needed. Strain into a serving vessel and serve immediately.

Note: Any juices from the plate where the meat rested should be added to the gravy.

Beef Tenderloin with Peppercorn Sauce

This steakhouse classic has been modified for the home kitchen, and makes a great choice for that next "fancy" special occasion dinner.

4 center-cut beef tenderloin filet mignon
steaks, about 8 oz each
Coarsely ground whole black peppercorns
Salt to taste
2 tbsps clarified butter, procedure below
2 tbsps finely minced shallots
½ cup brandy
1 cup veal stock or low-sodium beef broth
⅓ cup heavy cream
½ tsp Dijon mustard
3 drops Worcestershire sauce
1 tbsp cold unsalted butter

Salt the steaks generously on both sides. Set your pepper grinder to a coarse setting and very generously coat both sides of the steaks with pepper. You can also crush the peppercorns with the bottom of a heavy pot or skillet.

To clarify the butter: melt some butter and allow it to sit until the oils separate from the milk solids and water. Skim the milky foam from the surface and pour off the clarified butter being careful to not add the water at the bottom.

Add 2 tbsps of clarified butter to a large, heavy skillet. Place over high flame until very hot. Add the steaks and cook over medium high heat for about 4 minutes per side for medium-rare, or until desired doneness. Tranfer to a plate and cover loosely with foil.

Turn off the flame and deglaze the skillet with the brandy. Turn the heat back on high, and as soon as the brandy is almost evaporated, stir in the cream, veal stock, mustard, and Worcestershire, scraping the bottom of the skillet with a whisk to dissolve any meat juices caramelized on the bottom. Boil for a few minutes to reduce by half. Turn off the heat and whisk in the cold butter. Taste and adjust seasoning.

Place the steaks back in the hot sauce, tossing to coat. Serve immediately.

Stuffed Bell Peppers

This tasty cafeteria classic is the best use of leftover rice ever invented. You have to love a recipe where you get your meat, vegetable, and starch all in one delicious, beautiful package.

For the sauce...
1 tbsp olive oil
1 onion, sliced thin
1 cup beef broth
2½ cups prepared marinara sauce, or other tomato sauce
1 tbsp balsamic vinegar
¼ tsp red pepper flakes, optional

For the peppers...
1 lb lean ground beef
½ lb sweet Italian pork sausage, casings removed
2 cups cooked rice
1 cup of grated 'real' parmesan (Parmigiano Reggiano)
¼ cup chopped Italian parsley
4 cloves garlic, minced very fine
1 can (10 oz) diced tomatoes
2 tsps salt
1 tsp fresh ground black pepper
Pinch of cayenne
4 large red bell peppers

Pre-heat oven to 375°F.

Add the olive oil to a saucepan, and lightly brown the onions with a large pinch of salt over medium-high heat. Remove half and reserve for the stuffing. Stir in the rest of the sauce ingredients and bring to a simmer. Pour the sauce into the bottom of a large deep casserole dish.

Add all the filling ingredients to a mixing bowl, along with the reserved onions, and stir with a fork, or your hands, until the mixture is combined. Tip: you can cook a small piece of the filling to test the seasoning.

Cut the bell peppers in half lengthwise. Use a spoon to remove the stem, seeds and white membrane from each pepper. Place the bell peppers in the casserole dish, and fill each pepper with the stuffing. A little additional cheese can be grated over the top if desired.

Cover with foil and bake for 45 minutes. Remove foil and bake uncovered for another 20-30 minutes, or until the peppers are very tender. Exact cooking time will depend on size, shape and thickness of the peppers. Best to let rest for 10 minutes before serving. Serve with the sauce spooned over the top.

Prime Rib of Beef

A big, beautiful Prime rib is the ideal special occasion roast. This simple preparation shows off the lovely (and by lovely, I mean expensive) meat's best qualities – the deep, rich flavor, and juicy, buttery texture.

1 standing prime rib of beef roast (4 to 7 ribs, about 9 to 18 lbs), trimmed and tied
Room temperature butter, about ½ tbsp per rib bone
Fresh coarse-ground black pepper, as needed
Kosher salt (or other larger grain, flake-style salt), as needed
2 tbsps flour
4 cups cold beef broth, or veal stock if available
1 tbsp fresh chopped tarragon, optional

For the sauce...
6 tbsps creamed horseradish sauce
6 tbsps sour cream

Pre-heat oven to 450°F.

Place the prime rib in a large, sturdy metal roasting pan. No rack is needed as bones form a natural rack. Rub the entire surface of the roast with butter, and season very generously with kosher salt and black pepper. This is a big hunk of meat, so don't be shy with the seasoning. Leave the prime rib out at room temperature for 2 hours.

When the oven is hot, put the roast in for 20 minutes to sear the outside. After 20 minutes turn the oven down to 325°F., and roast until the desired internal temperature is reached (see below). Some use 15 minutes per pound as a rule of thumb, but a good digital thermometer is a much better idea.

The following are internal temperatures for removing the beef at, and not the final temperature. The meat will continue to cook after it's removed.

Rare: Remove at 110-115°F.
(Final temp about 120-125°F.)

Medium-Rare: Remove at 120-125°F.
(Final temp about 130-135°F.)

Medium: Remove at 130-135°F.
(Final temp about 140-145°F.)

Transfer to a serving platter, and let the prime rib rest, loosely covered with foil, for at least 30 minutes before slicing and serving. Cutting into the meat too early will cause a loss of juice, and self-esteem.

For the sauce: In a small bowl mix the horseradish sauce and sour cream together.

Serves 2 portions per rib

Slow-Roasted Pulled Pork With Kansas City Barbecue Sauce

The term "fork-tender" was invented for slow-roasted pork shoulder. Sure it takes half a day to make, but the building anticipation makes that first bite into the sticky, succulent meat even more special.

3½ to 4 lbs pork shoulder roast,
also called pork butt or Boston butt
1 tsp liquid smoke, optional

For the dry rub...
2 tbsps brown sugar
1 tbsp salt
1 tbsp freshly ground black pepper
1 tbsp paprika
2 tsps chile powder
2 tsps garlic powder
2 tsps onion powder
2 tsps ground cumin
1 tsp cayenne pepper

For the sauce...
2 cups ketchup
⅔ cup dark molasses
½ cup white vinegar
1 tsp paprika
1 tsp chili powder
1 tsp hot sauce
½ tsp freshly ground black pepper
½ tsp salt
½ tsp ground cinnamon
½ tsp ground allspice
½ tsp ground mace
½ tsp liquid smoke, optional

Pre-heat oven to 215°F.

Rinse the meat, and pat dry with paper towels. Trim off any large pieces of excess fat. Mix the rub ingredients together, and thoroughly coat all sides of the pork. Be sure to massage the rub into any folds in the meat.

Place the pork, fattier side up, in a large Dutch oven. Pour ⅓ cup water into a small, ovenproof ramekin, and add the liquid smoke. Place this ramekin in the Dutch oven next to the meat. As the pork roasts, this will introduce moisture to the cooking environment, as well as add a subtle smokiness to the meat. Cover tightly with the lid, and place in the center of the preheated oven.

Roast pork for 12 hours, or until very fork tender. If you're using a thermometer, the internal temperature will be around 200°F. Turn off the oven and allow the pork to rest for 1 hour before removing

To serve, place the pork on a cutting board and use two forks to pull it apart into small pieces. Some use a knife to chop the succulent meat, but legally you can no longer call it "pulled" pork. Taste for salt and spice level, and adjust the seasoning.

For the sauce: Whisk together the ingredients in a saucepan. Bring to a simmer over medium-low heat. Cook, stirring, for 3 minutes. Remove from heat, and let cool to room temperature before storing in an airtight container in the refrigerator. Served warm or room temperature as a condiment for grilled, roasted, and barbecued meats.

Serves 6-8

Ham Steaks
with caramalized apples

Applesauce is a natural with ham, even that stuff in the jar is pretty good with it, but when you use freshly sautéed apple slices it becomes a whole other experience.

¼ cup brown sugar
1 tbsp apple cider vinegar
1 cup apple cider or juice
Small pinch of cinnamon
2 tsps Dijon mustard
4 firm apples (Granny Smith, or any good cooking apple), peeled, cored, cut into quarters, and then each quarter into 4 slices (16 slices per apple).
3 tbsps unsalted butter, divided
Salt and freshly ground black pepper to taste
2 lbs ham steaks, cut into serving size pieces, or freshly baked ham slices

In a small bowl, whisk together the brown sugar, cider vinegar, apple cider or juice, cinnamon, and Dijon mustard. Reserve until needed. Prep the apples as directed.

Melt the 2 tbsps of the butter in a large skillet over high heat. As soon as the butter melts, wait half a minute and add the apples. Sauté for 3 to 4 minutes, or until the edges start to brown slightly.

Pour in the reserved mixture, turn the heat down to medium-high, and cook until the apples are tender and the liquid has reduced down to a glaze. If the liquid begins to get too thick before the apples are tender, just add a splash of water and continue cooking.

Taste and season with salt and freshly ground black pepper to taste. It may seem odd to add salt and black pepper to an apple sauce, but it's a very important flavor component.

Melt a tbsp of butter in the skillet, and gently warm the ham steaks over medium-low heat. Remember, the ham is already cooked, so you just want it warmed up, not re-cooked. Serve with the hot apples spooned over the top.

Serves 4-6

Roast Pork Tenderloin with Black Cherry Sauce

Not only is pork tenderloin very lean, it's is one of the easiest cuts of meat to cook. A sweet, tangy cherry sauce pairs perfectly with the pork's spicy black pepper crust.

2 trimmed pork tenderloins (about 1½ lbs each)
Kosher salt to taste
¼ cup coarsely ground black pepper
2 tbsps vegetable oil
1 clove garlic, crushed
⅓ cup balsamic vinegar
½ cup black cherry preserves
1 cup chicken stock
2 tbsps cold unsalted butter

Pre-heat oven to 375°F.

Coat all sides of the pork tenderloins generously with salt and black pepper, and to taste. Heat the vegetable oil, in a large, ovenproof frying pan, over medium-high heat, until it begins to smoke. Sear the pork on all sides, about 2 minutes per side. Turn off the heat; place the pan in the center of the preheated oven.

Roast the pork for about 25 minutes, or until the internal temperature reaches 140°F. for medium. When the pork is cooked, remove it from the pan to a plate and cover loosely with foil to rest while the sauce is made.

Pour off the excess fat from the frying pan, and place over high heat. Add the garlic and cook for just 15 seconds, then add the vinegar, cherry preserves, and chicken stock. Cook, scraping the bottom of the pan with a wooden spoon to deglaze the pan drippings.

Boil until the sauce reduces by about half, about 6 to 7 minutes. Turn off the heat, and whisk in the cold butter, stirring constantly until the butter disappears. Taste for salt, and adjust the seasoning. Slice the pork and serve with the sauce spooned over.

Serves 6

Barbecued Baby Back Ribs

It would be great if we all had a big ol' smoker in the backyard to make authentic barbecue with, but when done right, the oven does a surprisingly excellent job turning out tender, tasty ribs.

2 full racks baby back pork ribs, trimmed of excess fat, patted dry

For the rub...
⅓ cup packed light brown sugar
3 tbsps kosher salt
1 tsp ground black pepper
1 tbsp smoked or regular paprika
½ tsp ground chipotle pepper
½ tsp dried thyme
½ tsp dried mustard
½ tsp garlic powder
½ tsp onion powder
¼ tsp cayenne pepper

1½ cups Kansas City style barbecue sauce (Page 152)

Combine the spice rub ingredients in a small bowl and mix thoroughly. Place each rack of ribs in the center of its own large piece of heavy-duty aluminum foil. Generously apply the dry rub to each side of the two racks (more so on the meat side). Wrap each rack in foil; transfer to the refrigerator for at least 4 hours – overnight is even better.

Pre-heat oven to 250°F.

Place the two foil-wrapped racks on a baking sheet and place in oven. Bake for 2 hours. Remove the ribs from oven, and using tongs, carefully open the foil (excess fat can be poured off). Place both racks on one piece of the foil, and brush barbecue sauce generously on both sides.

Increase the oven temperature to 350°F.

Return pan of ribs to the oven. Continue cooking, brushing on more barbecue sauce several times, until the ribs are fork tender and well glazed, about 30 to 45 minutes.

Remove and let rest for 5 minutes before cutting and serving. Ribs can be tossed in additional sauce if desired, and/or served with extra sauce on the side.

Maple-Brined Roast Pork Loin with Mustard Glaze

Brining is a fantastic technique for a pork loin roast, since it keeps the lean meat very moist and flavorful. By the way, you can use this same brine recipe for a whole chicken, or turkey breast.

For the brine...
1 quart cold water
¼ cup salt
½ cup maple syrup
4 cloves garlic, crushed
1 tbsp cracked black pepper
2 tbsps chopped fresh rosemary leaves

3½ lbs boneless pork loin roast, trimmed
1 tbsp vegetable oil
Salt and freshly ground black pepper to taste

For the mustard crust...
⅓ cup maple syrup
3 tbsps Dijon mustard, or to taste
2 tbsps plain breadcrumbs
1 tbsp melted butter

Pre-heat oven to 450°F.

Pour the water into a plastic container, one with a lid, large enough to fit the pork. Add the salt, maple syrup, garlic, black pepper, and rosemary. Whisk together until the salt is dissolved. Add the pork loin roast. The pork should be fully submerged, so place a small plate on if necessary. Cover tightly and refrigerate overnight, or up to 24 hours.

Remove the pork from the brine, and pat dry with paper towels. Rub with the oil, season with salt and fresh ground black pepper. Place fatter side down, in a small roasting pan. Roast in oven for 15 minutes. While it roasts, mix the maple syrup and mustard in a small bowl. In a separate small bowl mix the breadcrumbs with the melted butter.

Remove, and turn down the oven to 325°F. Turn the pork over, so the fatter side is up, and spread on enough of the maple mustard mixture to generously coat the top (the rest of this mixture can be served at the table). Sprinkle over the buttered breadcrumbs.

Return to the oven and roast for another 45 to 60 minutes, or until the internal temp reaches 155°F.

Let rest for at least 15 minutes before slicing and serving along with any leftover maple mustard.

Smothered Pork Chops

This southern comfort classic features pan-fried pork chops covered in a simple, but super savory onion gravy. These are great over rice, which helps soak up the delicious sauce.

4 large pork chops, about 1½ inch thick
1 tsp poultry seasoning
Salt and fresh ground black pepper to taste
2 tbsps vegetable oil
1 tbsp butter
1 large yellow onion, sliced
4 cloves garlic, finely minced
1 rounded tbsp flour
1½ cup chicken broth
¼ cup buttermilk
¼ cup water
4 cups cooked rice, optional

Season pork chops on both sides with the poultry seasoning, salt and pepper. Heat the oil in a large frying pan over medium-high flame. When the oil is hot, brown the pork chops well, about 5 minutes per side. Remove from the pan and reserve on a plate.

Pour off the excess oil, and place the pan back on the stove over medium heat. Add the butter and the onions, along with a big pinch of salt. Sauté for about 10 minutes, or until the onions are well-browned. The onions need to caramelize for best results.

Stir in the garlic and cook for 1 minute. Stir in the flour and cook for 2 minutes. Add the chicken broth, buttermilk, and water. As the mixture comes to a simmer, use a wooden spoon to scrape any browned bits from the bottom of the pan.

Turn the heat to low, and let the onion gravy gently simmer for 15 minutes. Add a splash of water if it seems to be getting too thick. Add the pork chops and any juices back into the pan, and coat with the gravy. Cook for about 10 minutes, or until the pork reaches your desired level of doneness. Taste for seasoning and adjust if needed. Serve pork chops over rice, topped with the onion gravy.

Serves 4

Spaghetti & Meatballs

Did you know that spaghetti and meatballs is an American invention?
That's right, Italians don't believe in serving pasta and meatballs together.
Hey, they don't know what they're missing!

2 tbsps olive oil
1 yellow onion, diced fine
4 garlic cloves, minced
½ tsp dried Italian herbs
½ loaf day-old Italian bread, crust removed
¼ cup milk
2 lbs very cold ground beef
(recommend 80/20 lean/fat ratio)
2 tsps salt
1 tsp freshly ground black pepper
2 large eggs, beaten
⅓ cup chopped fresh Italian parsley
¾ cup freshly grated Parmigiano-Reggiano
cheese, plus more for service
6 cups marinara sauce, or other
prepared pasta sauce
1 cup water
Thick spaghetti (allow 4 oz uncooked per
person), cooked according to directions

Pre-heat oven to 425°F.

Heat the olive oil in a saucepan over medium-low heat; add the onion, garlic, and a pinch of salt. Sweat for 6 to 7 minutes, or until soft and golden. Turn off heat, stir in the dried Italian herbs, let cool to room temperature.

Tear the bread into small chunks and place into a food processor (work in batches depending on the size of the machine). Pulse on and off to make fine breadcrumbs. You'll need 2 cups total. Add the crumbs to a bowl and toss with the milk to moisten. Let sit 10 minutes.

In a large mixing bowl, use your hands to combine the beef, salt, black pepper, eggs, parsley, cheese, breadcrumbs, and cooled onion mixture.

Wet your hands and roll golf ball-size meatballs; arrange on an oiled sheet pan. Bake 20 minutes. While the meatballs are browning in the oven, bring the pasta sauce and water to a simmer. When the meatballs are done, transfer into the hot sauce. Turn heat to very low, cover, and simmer gently for 45 minutes.

When they're done, cook the spaghetti, drain well (never rinse), and add to a large pasta bowl. Ladle some of the sauce from the meatballs over the pasta and toss to coat. Serve the spaghetti topped with the meatballs, sauce, and freshly grated cheese.

Corned Beef & Cabbage

Corned beef and cabbage is the traditional St. Patrick's Day meal, but why only enjoy this easy recipe once a year?

3½ to 5 lbs corned beef brisket
Spice packet from the corned beef package
2 tsps coarsely ground black pepper
1 bay leaf
Salt as needed
2 lbs white potatoes, cut in quarters
4 carrots, peeled, cut in chunks
1 onions, large dice
3 stalks celery, large dice
1 small green cabbage, cored, cut in 8 wedges

Place the corned beef, 1 teaspoon of the salt, pepper, and spices into a large pot along with 3 quarts of cold water. Cover and bring to a boil over high heat. Turn down the heat to low and slowly simmer for 2½ hours.

Add the potatoes, carrots, onions, and celery. Simmer, covered for 20 minutes. Add the cabbage and cook covered for another 20 minutes, or until the potatoes and vegetables are tender. Remove the beef, and let rest 5 minutes. Slice against the grain and serve with the cabbage, potatoes, vegetables, and some of the cooking liquid. Serve with rye or dark bread and mustard on the side.

Braised Lamb Shanks

Only make this lamb shanks recipe if you like really enjoy flavorful, succulent, fork-tender meat.

6 lamb shanks, about 5½ lbs
2 tbsps olive oil
½ tsp dried rosemary
½ tsp dried thyme
Salt and fresh ground black pepper to taste
1 tbsp butter
1 onion, diced
1 rib celery, diced
1 large carrot, diced
1 tbsp flour
4 cloves garlic, minced
½ cup drinkable red wine
1 cup chicken broth
1 tbsp balsamic vinegar
½ cup water
⅛ tsp cinnamon
1 tsp minced fresh rosemary leaves

Pre-heat oven to 450°F.

Place the shanks in a deep, 15 x 10 inch baking dish, or similar sized roasting pan, large enough to fit the shanks in one layer. Rub with the olive oil, dried rosemary and thyme. Season generously with salt and pepper on both sides. Roast for 30 minutes to brown the lamb.

While the lamb is browning, place a saucepan on medium-high heat, and add the butter. When the butter foams, add the onion, celery, and carrot. Cook for about 6 to 7 minutes, or until the vegetables soften and the edges start to brown and caramelize.

Stir in the flour and cook for 1 minute. Add the garlic and cook for 1 minute more. Stir in the wine. When the wine comes to a boil, stir in the chicken broth, balsamic vinegar, water, and cinnamon. Bring back to a boil, turn off and reserve.

When the lamb has finished browning, remove, and turn the oven down to 325°F. Pour over the sauce mixture, and distribute evenly. Cover with heavy-duty foil, crimping the edges to form a tight seal. Roast for 1 hour, lift the foil, turn over the shanks, rewrap and cook for 1 more hour, or until fork tender.

Remove the lamb shanks to a large bowl, and cover with foil to keep warm.

Pour the braising liquid into a saucepan, and boil on high heat for 10 minutes, or until reduced by half and slight thickened. As the sauce reduces, the excess fat will pool up in the center of the pan and should be skimmed off with a ladle. Add the fresh rosemary, taste and adjust for seasoning. Transfer the lamb shanks to a serving platter, and serve topped with the sauce.

Makes 6

Grilled Lamb Chops with Orange Mint Jelly

These lamb rib chops are too gorgeous to cover in that bright green mint jelly from the supermarket. Making your own orange mint sauce is very easy, and so much better tasting.

3 cloves garlic, minced
2 tbsps olive oil
1 tsp cumin
½ tsp ground coriander
½ tsp black pepper
⅛ tsp cinnamon
½ tsp dried rosemary, crushed
½ tsp dried thyme
16 lamb rib chops (about 2½ lbs)
Salt to taste

For the mint sauce...
½ cup orange marmalade or jelly
1 tbsp rice wine vinegar
1 tbsp water
2 tbsps freshly chopped mint
¼ tsp red pepper flakes, optional
Pinch of salt

In a large baking dish, combine all the ingredients, except for the lamb chops and salt. Mix until combined, add the lamb chops and rub the marinade into both sides. Cover and refrigerate for 2 hours, turn over, and refrigerate for 2 hours more. Lamb chops may be marinated over night.

Combine all the sauce ingredients in a small mixing bowl. Refrigerate until needed.

Pre-heat grill, grill pan, or broiler. Remove chops from marinade and salt both sides generously. Cook about 3 minutes per side for medium-rare, or until desired doneness has been reached. Let rest for 5 minutes before serving with the mint sauce.

Serves 4

Whole Roast Garlic Herb Chicken with Pan Gravy

The only thing better than a fragrant, beautifully browned roast chicken is one served with a rich, freshly made pan gravy. The keys to this great recipe are a very hot oven and using a roasting pan you can also make the sauce in after the chicken is cooked.

1 large whole chicken, about 5 lbs, rinsed, dried with paper towels
4 cloves garlic
⅓ cup olive oil
2 tsps very finely minced fresh thyme leaves
2 tsps very finely minced fresh rosemary leaves
1 tsp dried Italian herbs
Salt and freshly ground black pepper to taste

For the gravy...
1½ tbsps reserved chicken fat
1 tbsp butter
1 heaping tbsp flour
2 cups cold chicken broth
½ tsp balsamic vinegar
4 sprigs fresh thyme
Salt and freshly ground black pepper to taste

Pre-heat oven to 450°F.

Remove skins and crush the garlic cloves with the flat of a knife. Mince and and press until it is a very fine paste.

Add olive oil, garlic, thyme, rosemary and dried Italian herbs to a large mixing bowl. Rub the chicken inside and out with the mixture. Continue or leave to marinade overnight or for a few hours.

Place chicken in an oven-proof skillet or roasting pan. Something that can be used on the stove flame later. Season the cavity with salt and freshly ground black pepper. Truss the legs with kitchen string.

Place in the centre of the oven and roast for one hour or until a thermometer registers 165°F. Remove the chicken, place on a platter and cover with foil. Allow to rest while making the gravy.

Pour the excess chicken fat from the pan, leaving 1½ tbsps behind, Place back on the stove and add the butter. When the butter melts add a little flour and cook, stirring with a whisk constantly until golden brown. Whisk in 2 cups of cold chicken broth, balsamic vinegar and thyme. Turn the heat to high, and boil for 5 minutes stirring until the gravy is thickened.

Serves 4

Chicken Parmesan Casserole with Tomato Sauce

Your dreams have been answered; America's favorite Italian-American chicken dish is now available in casserole form.

6 boneless skinless chicken breasts
(about 6 to 7 oz each)
2 tbsps olive oil
2 cloves garlic, finely minced
Hot red pepper flakes, to taste
4 cups marinara sauce
¼ cup chopped basil
8 oz shredded mozzarella, divided
4 oz grated Parmesan,
1 (5 oz) package garlic croutons

For the sauce...
¼ cup olive oil
1 onion, diced
1 rib celery, fine dice
4 cloves garlic, finely minced
1 tsp salt
2 tsps sugar
½ tsp dried Italian herbs
Pinch of red pepper flakes
1 tsp anchovy paste
1 tsp white wine vinegar
1 tbsp tomato paste
2 cans (28 oz) whole peeled San Marzano plum tomatoes, crushed by hand or food mill to a coarse puree
2 tbsps chopped fresh basil
Water as needed

Pre-heat oven to 350°F.

Place the chicken breasts on a plate and season both sides with salt and fresh ground black pepper. Set aside.

Spread the olive oil, garlic, and red pepper flakes evenly on the bottom of a 9 x 13 inch casserole dish. Add 1 cup of the marinara, and spread evenly. Place the chicken breasts in the dish, and space evenly so they cook uniformly. Top with the rest of the marinara sauce and basil.

Top with half the mozzarella, and half the Parmesan. Pour over the croutons and spread evenly. Top with the remaining cheese. Bake for 40 minutes, or until top is browned and the chicken is cooked through.

Let rest for 5 minutes before serving with some sauce spooned from the bottom of the casserole.

For the sauce: In a saucepan, sweat the onions and celery in the olive oil for 5 to 6 minutes, or until they begin to turn translucent. Add the garlic and cook for 1 minute more. Add the salt, sugar, dried herbs, pepper flakes, anchovy paste, vinegar, and tomato paste. Cook, stirring, for 2 minutes.

Add the tomatoes, bring to a simmer, turn down to low and simmer gently, stirring occasionally for 45 minutes. Water may be added to adjust thickness. Taste and adjust seasoning and reserve until needed.

Hunter's Chicken

Also commonly known as chicken cacciatore, this recipe's name is deliciously ironic. What kind of hunter is stalking and shooting chickens?

2 tbsps olive oil
8 large chicken thighs (about 3½ lbs)
Salt and fresh ground black pepper to taste
1 large onion, sliced
8 oz fresh mushrooms, thickly sliced
1 rounded tbsp flour
½ cup white wine
1½ cup chicken broth
1 cup crushed tomato
8 cloves garlic, peeled, left whole
3 springs fresh rosemary
1 bay leaf
1 tsp dried oregano
½ tsp red pepper flakes, or to taste
1 tsp salt
1 red bell pepper, sliced
1 green bell pepper, sliced

Pre-heat oven to 350°F.

Season the chicken generously with salt and freshly ground black pepper. Place a heavy Dutch oven on the stove over a medium-high heat; add the olive oil and brown the chicken thighs well on all both sides. Remove the chicken, and add the onions, and mushrooms. Reduce the heat to medium and sauté for about 5 minutes, until the onions soften.

Stir in the flour and cook for one minute. Stir in the wine, tomato, and chicken broth; bring to a boil, scraping the bottom with a wooden spoon to release the caramelized bits.

Add the garlic, rosemary, bay leaf, oregano, pepper flakes, and salt. Stir to combine. Place the chicken pieces, and any juices, over the sauce, and top with the sliced peppers. Cover with the lid and place in oven for 45 minutes. Remove the lid and roast for 15 minutes more

Remove from oven and let rest, covered for 10 minutes. Skim any excess fat from the top of the sauce. Taste and adjust seasoning. Serve over pasta, rice, or polenta.

Serves 4

Buttermilk Fried Chicken

The buttermilk not only keeps the chicken moist and tender, but it also helps create the irresistibly crisp, crunchy coating.

For the marinade...
**1 whole chicken (about 4 lbs),
cut in 8 serving size pieces
1 tsp salt
1 tsp black pepper
1 tsp paprika
½ tsp cayenne pepper
½ tsp white pepper
1 tsp poultry seasoning
2 cups buttermilk**

For the seasoned flour...
**2 cups all purpose flour
1 tbsp salt
1 tsp black pepper
1 tsp paprika
¼ tsp cayenne pepper
½ tsp white pepper
1 tsp garlic salt
1 tsp onion powder**

**2 quarts peanut oil, or vegetable
shortening for frying**

Place the chicken in a large glass bowl or plastic container. Add all the seasonings, and toss to coat very thoroughly. Pour over the buttermilk. Use tongs to move the chicken pieces around until they are coated. Cover and refrigerate for 6 to 12 hours.

Mix together the seasoned flour ingredients in a large baking dish. Drain the chicken pieces in a colander, and toss into the flour. Toss to coat the chicken completely with the flour mixture. Make sure it's thoroughly covered, including all the nooks and crannies. Gently shake off excess flour, and reserve on a plate.

Heat the oil or shortening in a heavy Dutch oven to 350°F. Carefully add the chicken and fry for 10 minutes. Use tongs or a wire strainer to turn the pieces over, and continue cook for another 8 to 10 minutes approximately, or until crisp, golden brown, and you've reached an internal temperature of 175°F to 180°F.

Remove to drain on a wire rack for 5 minutes before serving. May be sprinkled with additional salt and/or hot pepper if desired.

Makes 8

Chicken Pot Pie

You can make this in a casserole dish and serve it family-style, but there's something special about individual chicken pot pies. With these you always have that perfect balance between the thick, chunky filling, and the crisp, buttery crust.

1 tbsp olive oil
8 oz white button mushrooms, sliced
1 diced onion
2 cup sliced carrots
1 cup sliced celery
4 cups cold chicken broth, divided
6 tbsps butter
½ cup all-purpose flour
2 lbs skinless, boneless chicken breasts,
cut in 1 inch cubes
1 cup frozen green peas
1 tsp chopped fresh thyme leaves
or a pinch of dried
1 tsp salt
¼ tsp black pepper
1½ pounds pie dough (enough for 2 x 10inch pies)
6 large (15 oz) ramekins
1 egg, beaten

Pre-heat oven to 400°F.

In a large saucepan, sauté the mushrooms and onions in the olive oil over medium heat until golden. Add the carrots, celery, and 2 cups of chicken broth. Bring to a boil, reduce to low and simmer until the vegetables are almost tender.

Melt the butter in a large saucepan over medium heat. Whisk in the flour and cook, stirring, for 4 minutes, or until the flour is a light tan color and smells like cooked piecrust. Slowly whisk in 2 cups of cold chicken broth. Simmer over medium-low heat until the mixture thickens. Remove from heat, and reserve.

Add the vegetables and broth from the other pan when ready, and stir to combine. Add the chicken, peas, thyme, salt and pepper. Bring back to a simmer and cook, stirring, for 5 minutes. Taste for seasoning and set aside until needed.

Divide the pot pie filling between the 6 ramekins (you should fill up to ½ inch from the top). Cut out circles of pie dough 1 inch larger than the width of the ramekins. Place the dough over the pot pies. Go around each piece of dough, folding a ½ inch over to form a rim. If desired, pinch with your finger tips to form a crimped edge. Cut a small "X" in the center of each crust.

Place the ramekins on a sheet pan. Brush the tops with the beaten egg. Bake for 35 to 40 minutes, or until pies are golden brown and bubbly. Cool for 15 minutes before serving.

Barbecue-Glazed Chicken Legs

What's more fun to eat than a tasty chicken drumstick? A tasty chicken drumstick covered with a thick, glistening barbecue glaze.

12 chicken drumsticks, about 3½ lbs
1 cup barbecue sauce, divided
1 tbsp brown sugar
1 tbsp cider vinegar
1 tsp salt, plus more as needed
½ tsp freshly ground black pepper
½ tsp hot sauce
Vegetable oil to grease pan

Pre-heat oven to 400°F.
(See page 152 for the barbecue sauce recipe)

With a sharp knife, make 2 slashes, about 1 inch apart into the thickest part of the drumstick, cutting to the bone. Transfer the chicken to a large sealable plastic freezer bag.

In a small bowl, mix together ¼ cup of the barbecue sauce with the rest of the ingredients. Pour into the bag of chicken, press out most of the air, and seal tightly. Shake the bag gently to distribute the sauce evenly. Refrigerate for at least 4 hours.

Line a baking sheet with foil and grease lightly with vegetable oil. Remove the chicken from the bag with tongs and space evenly on the pan. Discard the contents of the bag. Brush both sides of the drumsticks with barbecue sauce.

Bake for 15 minutes, remove, and brush generously with more sauce. Return to the oven, and repeat this process 3 more times for a total cooking time of 1 hour. When done, the chicken will be cooked through and be sporting a thick beautiful glaze.

Chicken and Mushroom Marsala over Garlic Toasts

Chicken Marsala is very popular in Italian-American restaurants, and usually calls for chicken to be pounded out thin, and dredged in flour before cooking. This home adaptation uses whole breasts for a moister, easier version. When buying the wine, be sure to get regular Marsala, not the sweet dessert style.

4 thick slices Italian or French bread
Olive oil as needed
1 whole garlic clove
4 large boneless chicken breasts, skin on
Salt and freshly ground black pepper to taste
2 tbsps olive oil
8 large white mushrooms, sliced
2 tbsps finely minced shallot
2 cloves garlic, minced fine
1½ tbsps flour
1½ cup Marsala wine
2 cups chicken broth
2 tbsps cold butter, cut in small pieces
1 tbsp freshly chopped parsley

Lightly brush the bread slices with olive oil, and toast under a broiler until golden brown on both sides. Remove and rub the whole garlic clove enthusiastically over the toasted surface of each slice. Set aside until needed.

Season the chicken breasts on both sides generously with salt and pepper. Heat the olive oil in a large skillet over medium-high flame. Place the chicken skin-side down and sear for 5 minutes. Turn over and cook for another 5 minutes, or until just cooked through. Remove to a plate and reserve while you make the sauce.

Add the mushrooms, and a pinch of salt to the pan, reduce the heat to medium and cook the mushrooms until they begin to soften and give up their juices. Continue cooking until the liquid evaporates and the mushrooms begin to brown. Add the shallots and garlic; cook, stirring,1 minute. Add the flour; cook, stirring, for 2 minutes.

Carefully add the Marsala (it may flame up which is fine), turn up the heat to high, and cook, stirring, for 2 minutes. While it cooks, scrape the bottom of the pan with a whisk to deglaze any of the caramelized bits. Add the chicken broth and boil until the sauce begins to reduce and thicken slightly.

Reduce the heat to very low, and add the chicken breasts back into the pan, tossing them in the sauce to coat and re-heat. Turn off the heat, and plate each chicken breast on top of a slice of toasted bread. Add the parsley, and butter to the sauce and whisk until butter disappears. Adjust seasoning with salt and pepper to taste. Spoon the sauce over the top and serve immediately.

Serves 4

King Ranch Chicken Casserole

*The flavors in this easy chicken casserole are as big as Texas,
the state where this hearty dish was born.*

1 cup of chicken broth
1 can cream of mushroom soup
1 can cream of chicken soup
1 (10 oz) can diced tomatoes with green chilies
2 tbsps sour cream
1 white onion, diced small
1 red bell pepper, diced small
1 green bell pepper, diced small
2 jalapeño, seeded, diced fine, optional
2 tsps ancho chile powder
2 tsps cumin
1½ tsps salt
½ tsp dried oregano
½ tsp chipotle chile powder, or to taste
Meat from one cooked chicken, roughly shredded
8 oz sharp cheddar cheese, grated, divided
8 to 10 corn tortillas, quartered

Pre-heat oven to 350°F.

Combine the chicken broth, soups, tomatoes, sour cream, onions, peppers, and spices in a mixing bowl and stir to combine thoroughly. Once mixed, spoon ½ cup of the sauce into a separate bowl and reserve for the top of the casserole.

Place half the chicken in a lightly-oiled 9 x 13 casserole dish. Spoon over half the sauce mixture, and spread evenly. Top with a third of the cheese. Top with half the tortillas. There is no need to overlap the tortilla pieces. A single layer is fine.

Top with the rest of the chicken, and then spread over the rest of the sauce. Top with the next third of the cheese, then the rest of the tortillas to cover the surface completely. Use a spatula to spread over the ½ cup of reserved sauce. Top with the last third of the cheese.

Bake uncovered for 40 minutes, or until golden brown and bubbly. Let rest for 15 minutes before serving.

Old Fashioned Chicken and Dumplings

This is one of America's ultimate comfort foods. Some folks like their dumplings light and airy, while others prefer them more hearty and dense. These are somewhere in between, but every bit as delicious.

2 tbsps vegetable oil
1 whole chicken (4 to 5 lbs is ideal),
cut in quarters, backbone reserved
1 quart chicken broth
3 cups water
4 cloves garlic, peeled
1 bay leaf
4 springs fresh thyme
5 tbsps butter
2 carrots, cut into ½ inch pieces
2 ribs celery, cut into ½ inch pieces
1 large onion, chopped
5 tbsps flour
1½ tsp salt
Freshly ground black pepper to taste
Dash of hot sauce

For the dumplings...
1¾ cups all-purpose flour
1 tsp salt
2 tsps baking powder
¼ tsp baking soda
3 tbsps cold butter
2 tbsps thinly sliced green onion tops
¼ cup buttermilk
¾ cup milk

Place a Dutch oven on the stove over high heat. Brown the chicken pieces and add broth, water, garlic, bay leaf and thyme. Boil and then turn heat down and simmer covered for 30 minutes. After 30 minutes, uncover, remove chicken to a bowl to cool. Strain the cooking liquid into a separate bowl, skimming off any fat that rises to the top.

Place the Dutch oven on a medium heat on the stove and add butter, carrots, celery and onion. Sauté for 5 minutes before carefully stirring in the flour. Cook for 2 minutes and then whisk in the reserved cooking liquid one cup at a time. Add salt, pepper and hot sauce. Reduce the heat to low and simmer covered for 30 minutes until the vegetables are tender.

Remove the chicken meat from the bones and tear into chunks. Stir the chicken pieces into the cooked vegetables. Cover with a lid and reduce heat to lowest possible temperature.

To make the dumplings: Add flour, salt, baking powder and baking soda into a mixing bowl. Stir. Add the cold butter and cut in using a pastry blender until the mixture is coarse crumbs. Add the green onions, buttermilk and milk and stir with a fork into a thick dough.

Turn the heat on the Dutch oven to medium, stir and drop large balls of the dumpling dough into the mixture. Cover and cook for 15 minutes. The dumplings are done when they are firm and cooked in the middle. Turn off the heat and serve.

Grilled Chipotle Lime Chicken Breasts

This brightly flavored southwestern-style recipe is the perfect antidote for the boring boneless, skinless chicken breast.

6 large boneless skinless chicken breasts
¼ cup fresh lime juice
¼ cup orange juice
4 cloves of garlic, crushed fine
1½ tsps chipotle chile powder
1 tsp smoked paprika
1 tsp cumin
2 tbsps vegetable oil
Fresh lime wedges, optional
Salt to taste

Use a sharp knife to score the top of the chicken breast in a crisscross pattern with ⅛ inch deep cuts, spaced about every half inch.

Add all the ingredients except the chicken and salt into a mixing bowl. Whisk to combine thoroughly. Add the chicken and toss to coat. Pour the contents into a large zip top plastic freezer bag, seal, and marinade in the refrigerator for between 3 and 6 hours.

Remove the chicken breasts to a plate. Pat the chicken lightly with paper towel to remove some excess liquid. Brush with a little vegetable oil, and season generously with salt. If so desired, more chipotle may be added at this point for a spicier version.

Cook the breasts on a preheated charcoal grill for 5 to 7 minutes per side, or until cooked through. These may also be done on a gas grill, or a stovetop grill pan. Serve the chicken breasts topped with wedges of fresh lime if desired.

Chicken Fettuccini Alfredo

This Italian-American restaurant favorite is easy to make at home, and this recipe doesn't use butter, and replaces some of the cream with chicken broth for a slightly lighter, but just as delicious version. Do not make this unless you have the real Parmigiano-Reggiano cheese!

2 cups low sodium chicken broth
2 large chicken breasts
2 cups heavy cream
4 cloves garlic, very finely minced
2 large egg yolks
¼ cup chopped Italian parsley
2 cups freshly grated Parmesan cheese (you must use real Parmigiano-Reggiano cheese)
Salt and freshly ground black pepper to taste
1 lb fettuccini

Bring the chicken breasts and broth to a simmer in a small saucepan over medium heat. Cover, reduce the heat to low and simmer for 12 minutes. Turn off the heat and let sit in the hot broth for 15 minutes. When the chicken has cooled, cut into thin slices and reserve.

Put the pasta water on to boil.

Bring the chicken broth back to a boil over high heat. Cook until the broth has reduced by half. Add the cream and garlic and when the mixture comes to a simmer, reduce the heat to low.

Beat the eggs in a small bowl. Slowly whisk in a half-cup of the hot cream mixture to warm the eggs. Turn off the heat and whisk the egg mixture into the cream sauce. Stir in 1 cup of the Parmesan cheese, and the parsley. Season with salt and freshly ground black pepper to taste. Stir in the sliced chicken. Cover and reserve.

Boil the fettuccini in salted water according to directions. Drain well, but do not rinse. Quickly return the hot pasta back into the pot, and pour over the sauce. Stir well with a wooden spoon, cover, and let sit 1 minute. Remove the cover, stir in the last cup of the Parmesan cheese, and let sit for one more minute. Serve hot topped with additional grated cheese.

Note: In the summer replace the parsley with some nice fresh basil.

Roast Turkey Breast with Cranberry Sauce

By taking the breast off the bone, you'll get an easier to cook roast, and a much prettier presentation. Any fresh herbs from the garden will work in this recipe.

1 bone-in turkey breast half,
about 3 lbs kitchen twine

For the herb rub...
2 tbsps soft butter
2 tbsps good olive oil
1 tsp lemon juice
1 finely minced garlic clove
1 tbsp chopped fresh parsley
1 tsp chopped fresh thyme leaves
1 tsp chopped fresh rosemary leaves
¼ tsp dried sage, or poultry seasoning
Salt and fresh ground black pepper to taste

For the sauce...
1 lb fresh or thawed frozen cranberries
1 tbsp grated orange zest
⅔ cup freshly squeezed orange juice
½ cup light brown sugar
¼ cup white sugar
Pinch of salt
⅔ cup water

For the sauce: Put the cranberries in a heavy-bottom pan with the orange zest and juice, sugar, and the water. Bring to a boil, then reduce the heat and simmer for 12 to 15 minutes, until the cranberries have burst. Remove from the heat. Allow to cool to room temperature before refrigerating. Serve cold or room temperature.

Pre-heat oven to 425°F.

Add the herb spread ingredients to a small bowl, and whisk to combine. Use a boning knife to remove the breast from the breastbone and ribcage (or have the butcher do it). Place the breast, skin side down, on the cutting board. Fold the tenderloin toward the thinner side of the breast. Use the boning knife to make a slice into the thickest part of the breast, creating a shallow flap. Be careful not to cut all the way through, we just want some extra surface area for the herb rub.

Season very generously with salt and fresh ground black pepper. Rub on the herb spread. Fold the tenderloin back over into the center of the breast and gather together.

Take a piece of kitchen twine and tie a simple square knot around the breast at the thickest point. Repeat this every inch or so, until the breast is trussed into a nice, round, tight package. Flip over, skin side up, and place in a lightly oiled shallow roasting pan. Rub any leftover herb rub over the skin, and season with salt and fresh ground black pepper to taste.

Roast the turkey for 20 minutes, then reduce the heat to 325°F. and continue roasting until a thermometer registers 165°F. when inserted into the thickest area of the breast (about 45 mins).

When the turkey's done, cover loosely with foil and let rest for 15 minutes before slicing and serving with any juices that collected in the pan. Serve with chilled cranberry sauce.

Serves 4

Turkey Cutlets

These crispy cutlets are fast to make, and very addictive to eat. A squeeze of fresh lemon is all you really need, but these will work nicely with gravy, tartar sauce, or even barbecue sauce.

1½ cups all-purpose flour
1 tsp garlic powder
1 tsp onion powder
¼ tsp cayenne pepper
4 large eggs
4 cups Japanese-style panko breadcrumbs,
or more as needed
2 lbs turkey cutlets, sliced or pounded to an
even ¼ inch thickness
Salt and freshly ground black pepper to taste
1 tsp poultry seasoning
Canola oil for frying
Lemon wedges

Add the flour, garlic powder, onion powder, and cayenne into a shallow dish. Stir thoroughly to combine; reserve. Whisk the eggs in a mixing bowl; reserve. Pour the breadcrumbs into a shallow baking dish; reserve.

Season the turkey cutlets on both sides generously with the salt and freshly ground black pepper to taste, and dust lightly with the poultry seasoning.

Dredge the turkey cutlets in the seasoned flour. One or two at a time, dip the cutlets into the egg, and once coated, transfer into the breadcrumbs. Turn over several times, pressing lightly in the crumbs to make sure the meat is thoroughly coated. Transfer cutlets to a pan, and continue until they're all breaded. When done breading, let rest for 15 minutes before frying.

Pour about ¼ inch of oil into a large, heavy skillet (ideally cast iron) and set over medium high heat. When the oil is hot enough to fry (350°F. or test with a small piece of breading), cook for about 2 to 3 minutes per side, or until golden brown and cooked through.

Work in batches, drain on paper towels or wire rack, and keep in a warm oven (175°F.) until all are done. Serve immediately with lemon wedges, or other sauce of your choice.

Crispy Duck Legs with Sweet & Sour Apricot Sauce

Do yourself a favor and ask your butcher to get you some duck legs. They're better value than breast or whole duck, and very simple to cook. You can serve one as a first course, or two for an entrée. This recipe can be easily doubled, just use a large roasting pan instead of a skillet to cook the duck after browning.

1 tbsp olive oil
6 duck legs, trimmed
Salt and fresh ground black pepper to taste
1 yellow onion, sliced
1 carrot, sliced
1 rib celery, sliced
6 whole garlic cloves, bruised
6 sprigs fresh thyme
1 cup chicken broth

For the sauce...
1 cup apricot preserves
2 tbsps rice vinegar
1 tbsp water
1 tsp fresh thyme leaves
Salt to taste
Coarsely-ground black pepper to taste

Pre-heat oven to 325°F.

Season the duck legs on both sides generously with salt and fresh ground black pepper. Heat the olive oil in a large oven-proof skillet, over medium flame, and place in the duck legs, skin side down. Cook until the duck skin is well-browned, about 6 to 7 minutes. Turn over and brown the meat side for 3 minutes.

Remove legs to a plate, pour off the excess fat, and add the vegetables, garlic, and thyme. Arrange the legs over the vegetables, skin side up. Pour in the broth, cover with foil, and place the skillet in the oven.

Roast for 1 hour and 15 minutes, or until the meat is almost fork tender. Uncover, and turn the oven up to 425°F. Roast another 20 minutes, or until the duck is tender and the skin is crisp. Let rest for 10 minutes before serving topped with the apricot sauce.

For the sauce: Add the preserves, rice vinegar, and water to a small saucepan. Bring to a simmer, stirring, over medium heat. Remove from heat and stir in the thyme, black pepper, and salt to taste. Serve warm or room temperature.

Spice-Rubbed Seared Tuna Steaks with Balsamic Reduction

These seared-on-the-outside, rare-in-the-middle tuna steaks are a very popular restaurant offering these days, and quite easy to do at home. The sharp, intensively flavored balsamic reduction is a perfect foil for the buttery texture and rich, meaty taste.

1½ lbs center-cut Ahi tuna fillet
1½ tsps kosher salt
1 tsp ground coriander
1 tsp paprika
¼ tsp cayenne pepper
1½ tbsps coarse black pepper, freshly ground
2 tbsps vegetable oil
4 lemon wedges, optional garnish

For the reduction...
6 tbsps aged balsamic vinegar
1 lemon, juiced
1 garlic clove, peeled, halved

Place the balsamic vinegar, lemon juice, and garlic in a small saucepan on the stove over medium-low heat. Simmer until the mixture reduces by half. Turn off the heat and reserve until needed. This sauce does not have to be hot for service. The reduction will thicken slightly as it cools.

Slice the tuna fillet into 4 equal size rectangular steaks. In a small bowl, combine the salt, coriander, paprika, and cayenne. Lay the tuna steaks out on a plate, and sprinkle the spice mixture evenly on all sides.

Evenly coat the tuna steaks with the freshly ground black pepper, and gently press it in, so that it adheres to the surface, being careful not to smash the flesh.

Place a thick-bottomed frying pan, or cast iron skillet on the stove over medium-high heat. Add the oil and swirl to coat the pan. When you see small wisps of smoke, add the tuna to the pan and sear the steaks for about 1 minute per side, or until desired doneness is reached.

Remove to a cutting board. For presentation, cut each steak diagonally into 4 to 5 slices and fan on a plate. Serve with a small amount of sauce drizzled along side. Garnish with additional lemon if desired.

Note: Seared Ahi tuna is best cooked rare to achieve its wonderfully meaty flavor and buttery texture. Overcooking will make it dry and "fishier" tasting.

Serves 4

Grilled Salmon Fillet with Fresh Mango Salsa

Mango salsa is a very popular topping for grilled salmon in restaurants, but not as common at home, which is a shame since it's so easy to do well. The tropical and tangy topping is a perfect match with smoky fish.

6 (6 to 7 oz) salmon fillets, boneless and skinless
2 tsps kosher salt
2 tsps vegetable oil

For the Mango Salsa...
1 ripe mango, peeled, seeded, and diced small (about 1½ cups)
2 tbsps red bell pepper, finely diced
2 tbsps red onion, finely diced
1 tbsp finely diced jalapeño
2 tbsps fresh lime juice
2 tbsps chopped fresh cilantro
1 tbsp rice vinegar
1 tbsp olive oil
¼ tsp cumin
Pinch of cayenne, optional
Salt to taste
Lime wedges to garnish

In a mixing bowl, combine all the mango salsa ingredients and set aside. Let sit out at room temperature for 30 minutes before serving. Toss before using.

Brush salmon lightly with the vegetable oil, and season generously on all sides with the salt. Preheat grill to medium-high. Grill the salmon for 5 to 7 minutes per side until lightly charred, and cooked to your desired doneness. Serve with the mango salsa, lime wedges, and salt.

Serves 6

Drunken Mussels

This is probably the easiest shellfish recipe ever. The mussels are quickly steamed in an aromatic wine broth, and in minutes you're ready to enjoy. Be sure to have some grilled bread around so as not to waste any of the delicious juices.

4 tbsps butter
4 cloves garlic, sliced thin
1 shallot, thinly sliced
1½ cups white wine
¼ cup chopped fresh Italian parsley
½ tbsp lemon zest
Pinch of red pepper flakes, optional
3 lbs fresh mussels, scrubbed and rinsed
Lemon wedges, optional

Add the butter to a large stockpot (one with a tight-fitting lid). Melt it over medium heat, and add the garlic and shallots; cook for one minute, or until they begin to sizzle.

Add the wine, parsley, lemon zest, and pepper flakes. Turn the heat to high and bring the mixture to a boil. Add the mussels and cover quickly. Cook for 3 minutes, give the pot a little shake back and forth, and cook for another 2 to 4 minutes, or until the mussels have opened.

As soon as the shells open, serve immediately. The mussels will shrivel up to nothing if left to simmer in the hot liquid. Divide among some deep bowls. Taste the broth for salt (usually the mussels provide enough natural salt, but add some if needed). Ladle some of the broth over each bowl, and dig in. Serve with extra lemon wedges if desired.

Halibut Steaks with Spinach & Warm Bacon Dressing

A warm spinach salad with the traditional, sweet and sour bacon dressing is always a special treat, but it also makes a great bed for pan-grilled halibut.

4 (6 oz) halibut steaks or fillets
Salt and freshly ground black pepper to taste
2 tsps vegetable oil
4 handfuls (about 12 oz) baby spinach, washed and dried
½ cup cherry tomato halves
4 lemon wedges

For the dressing...
4 strips bacon, cut in small pieces
1 tbsp olive oil
½ cup cider vinegar
4 tsp sugar
2 tsps lemon juice
½ tsp dry mustard
⅛ tsp freshly ground black pepper
Pinch of salt

Add the olive oil to a saucepan and cook the bacon over medium heat until crisp. Turn off the heat. Remove and reserve the bacon pieces, leaving the fat in the pan. Whisk in the rest of the dressing ingredients, and reserve. The dressing does not have to be emulsified, as it will be brought to a boil before serving.

Brush the halibut with the vegetable oil and season generously with salt and freshly ground black pepper. Preheat a cast iron grill pan over medium high heat, and grill the halibut for about 4 minutes per side, or until the desired doneness is reached.

While the halibut is cooking, add the spinach and cherry tomatoes to a large mixing bowl. When the fish is close to being done, bring the dressing to a boil, whisking, and pour over the spinach. Toss with tongs until the leaves are evenly coated and slightly wilted. Divide onto four plates.

Top with the cooked halibut. Finish with the reserved crisp bacon and a wedge of lemon.

Note: This is also wonderful with salmon, and if you like, thinly sliced mushrooms can be added to the spinach.

Egg-Dipped Sole Filet "Dore"

This simple and very quick egg batter keeps the fish really moist, and gives it a beautiful golden brown color. A great fish recipe for large groups.

2½ lbs petrale sole filets
Salt and freshly ground black pepper to taste
1½ cups flour
4 eggs, beaten
4 tbsps unsalted butter
6 lemon wedges

Pat sole filets dry with paper towels, and season both sides with salt and fresh ground black pepper to taste. Place the flour in a baking dish, and the beaten eggs in another. Dredge the seasoned fish filets, one at a time in the flour, coating both sides thoroughly, and then transfer into the dish of eggs. As they're added, turn the sole filets in the egg to coat both sides, and leave in the egg.

Once all the sole filets are floured and in the eggs, refrigerate until needed. In a large non-stick skillet, cook the butter over medium heat, until the foam disappears. Lift the sole filets out of the egg mixture, allowing the excess to drip off, and sauté in the butter for about 2 minutes per side until golden brown. Cook in batches if necessary, and keep warm in a very low oven. Serve on warm plates with lemon wedges.

Optional Lemon Butter Sauce: When all the sole is cooked, turn off the pan, and add the juice from one lemon, and 2 tbsps of cold butter. Whisk until the butter melts. Season, and spoon over the fish.

SEAFOOD • EGG-DIPPED SOLE FILET "DORE"

Broiled Rainbow Trout
with Lemon Parsley Brown Butter

One of the simplest of all seafood accompaniments, this classic brown butter sauce is perfect with mild-flavored trout.

6 whole boneless rainbow trout
Salt and freshly ground black pepper to taste
6 tbsps unsalted butter
3 tbsps fresh lemon juice
¼ cup chopped fresh parsley
Lemon wedges to garnish

Place the butter in a saucepan over medium-low heat. Cook until the butter turns a golden brown color, and takes on a nutty aroma. Reduce heat to very low and keep warm.

Remove the heads from the trout, and place skin-side-down on lightly-greased foil-lined baking sheets. Lightly brush a little of the browned butter over the surface. Season generously with salt and fresh ground black pepper.

Broil about 4 inches from the flame for about 3 to 5 minutes, or until fish flakes when tested with a fork. While the fish is cooking, turn the butter up to medium heat and whisk in the lemon juice. As soon as the mixture comes to a boil, add the parsley, turn off the heat.

When ready, serve the trout on warm plates with the hot lemon parsley brown butter spooned over the top. Serve lemon wedges on the side.

Serves 6

Wild Salmon Cakes with Tarragon Aioli

Not only is it perfect for a recipe like this, but canned salmon is wild-caught, and nutritionally superior to fresh farmed salmon.

1 (15 oz) can red or pink salmon
(or 2 cups flaked, fresh-cooked salmon)
⅓ cup plain dry breadcrumbs, plus more as needed
1 large egg, beaten
1 tbsp mayonnaise
1 tbsp capers, chopped
1 tbsp fresh lemon juice
1 clove garlic, crushed, minced fine
1 tsp fresh tarragon, chopped fine
½ tsp Dijon mustard
½ tsp salt
¼ tsp black pepper
2 tbsps olive oil
1 tbsp butter
Fresh lemon wedges to garnish

To serve...
½ tsp Dijon mustard
2 tbsps mayonnaise
2 tbsps sour cream
2 tsps fresh tarragon, chopped very fine
1 tsp lemon juice
Pinch of cayenne
Pinch of salt

Combine all the sauce ingredients in a small bowl and whisk to combine. Refrigerate until needed.

Add the salmon to a mixing bowl, along with ⅓ cup breadcrumbs and the rest of the ingredients, except the oil and butter. Mix with a fork until thoroughly combined. Refrigerate for 30 minutes.

Shape into 6 patties about an inch thick, and place on a plate lightly dusted with breadcrumbs. Dust the tops of the salmon cakes lightly with breadcrumbs also. Heat the oil and butter in a large skillet over medium heat until the butter melts. Cook the salmon cakes for about 3 to 4 minutes per side, or until golden brown and heated through. Serve hot with the sauce and fresh lemon.

Makes 6

Garlic Shrimp Angel Hair

Angel hair pasta is perfect for soaking up this very light, but very garlicky sauce. Together they make a great base for the sweet, freshly sautéed shrimp.

2 lbs raw, peeled and deveined shrimp, shells reserved
3 tbsps butter
3 cups water
¼ cup olive oil
Salt to taste
¼ cup freshly minced garlic
½ cup diced tomatoes
½ cup cream
1 lemon, juiced
¼ tsp red chili flakes, or to taste
3 tbsps chopped Italian parsley
1 (14 oz) package dry angel hair pasta
6 lemon wedges, optional

To make the shrimp stock: Place the shrimp shells in a saucepan, along with 1 tbsp of butter, and place over medium heat. Sauté the shells for about 4 minutes, then add 3 cups of water. Bring to a simmer, reduce heat to low, and simmer for 25 minutes. Strain and reserve stock until needed.

Place a pot of salted water on to boil for the pasta.

Add the olive oil to a large skillet over high heat. Season the shrimp with salt. As soon as the oil in the pan is hot and begins to shimmer, add the shrimp and sauté for 3 to 4 minutes, until they just turn pink. Remove to a bowl with a slotted spoon, leaving the olive oil in the pan. Reserve the shrimp until needed.

Add 2 tbsps of butter to the skillet and sauté the garlic over medium-low heat for about 2 minutes. Do not brown the garlic. Add the tomatoes, shrimp stock, and cream. Turn the heat to high, and bring the mixture to a boil, scraping the bottom with a wooden spoon to release any caramelized bits. Cook until reduced by half, about 10 minutes. Turn the heat down to low, and keep warm until needed.

Cook the angel hair pasta 1 minute less than the package states. Drain into a colander. While the pasta is draining, add the shrimp to the sauce, along with the lemon juice, chili flakes, and parsley. The shrimp will only take a few minutes to heat through.

Transfer the pasta back into the pot, and pour over the shrimp and sauce. Stir to combine, and let sit for one minute to absorb the sauce. Taste for salt, and then use tongs to divide the angel hair between the 6 plates. Using a spoon, divide the shrimp and sauce over the top of the pasta. Serve hot with lemon wedges if desired.

San Francisco Cioppino

There are two ways to make Cioppino – the way you do it, and the wrong way. This spicy fish stew just begs to be adapted to your personal tastes. Whether you make yours thick, thin, spicy or mild, just be sure to have lots of crusty sourdough bread around to soak up the sauce!

2 tbsps olive oil
2 tbsps butter
1 rib celery, finely diced
1 onion, diced
6 cloves garlic, finely minced
2 cups good white wine
1 bay leaf
½ tsp dried oregano
½ tsp dried basil
½ tsp red pepper flakes, or to taste
½ tsp Worcestershire sauce
1 can (28 oz) tomato puree, or whole plum tomatoes, crushed fine
3 cups clam juice, fish stock, or water, plus more as needed to adjust thickness
1 tsp salt, or to taste
5 to 6 thin slices of lemon
1 cooked Dungeness crab (about 2 lbs), cracked and cleaned, or 1 lb frozen crabmeat, thawed
12 oz fresh cod, any other white fish, cut into 1 inch pieces
1 lb raw shrimp, peeled and deveined
1 lb fresh mussels, scrubbed
¼ cup chopped Italian parsley

Add the butter and olive oil to a large pot, and place on the stove over a medium-low heat. Add the celery and onions with a pinch of salt, and sauté them until soft, about 7 minutes. Add the garlic and sauté for one minute. Add the wine, turn the heat up to high, and bring to a boil.

Add the bay leaf, oregano, basil, pepper flakes, Worcestershire, tomato puree and clam juice. When the mixture comes back to a boil, reduce the heat to low and simmer uncovered for 45 minutes. Add water if the sauce gets too thick.

Turn the heat to high, and when the sauce returns to a rapid boil, add the remaining ingredients, stir, cover tightly, and cook for 5 minutes, or until the mussels open. Turn off the heat, taste for salt and spiciness, and adjust if needed.

Ladle ciopinno into large bowls and serve with lots of sourdough bread to soak up the sauce. Bonus points if you find some Anchor Steam beer and enjoy cioppino like a real San Franciscan.

Shrimp & Grits

When you think comfort food, you probably don't think of shrimp, but this great dish from South Carolina's "Lowcountry" may change your mind.

For the grits...
1 cup white grits
4 cups water
2 tbsps butter
1 tsp salt
½ cup grated white cheddar

For the shrimp...
4 strips bacon, cut in ¼ inch pieces
1 lb large shrimp (16 to 20 per/lb), peeled and deveined
½ tsp Cajun seasoning
¼ tsp salt
¼ tsp black pepper
Pinch of cayenne
⅓ cup water or chicken stock
2 tbsps cream
2 tsps lemon juice
Dash of Worcestershire sauce
3 cloves garlic, minced fine
2 tbsps minced green onions
1 tbsp minced jalapeno
1 tbsp chopped parsley

Cook the bacon in a large skillet over medium heat until almost crisp. Turn off the heat. Remove the bacon with a slotted spoon and reserve. Leave about 1 tbsp of bacon fat in the pan; set aside

To cook the grits: In a medium saucepan, bring the water, butter, and salt to a boil. Whisk in the grits, and reduce heat to low. Cook, stirring occasionally, until smooth and creamy, about 20 minutes. Turn off the heat and stir in the cheese. Cover and reserve until the shrimp are done.

To cook the shrimp: Mix the water, cream, lemon juice, and Worcestershire in a small bowl and set aside. Add the shrimp, Cajun seasoning, salt, black pepper, and cayenne to a mixing bowl. Toss with a spatula until the shrimp are coated evenly with the seasonings.

Turn the heat back on high under the skillet. When you see the first wisp of smoke, quickly add the shrimp mixture. Use tongs to distribute the shrimp into a single layer. Turn the heat down medium-high and cook for 1 minute. Turn the shrimp over and cook for 1 minute more. Add the garlic, green onions, jalapeno, and reserved bacon, cook, stirring, 2 minutes. Add the liquid mixture and cook, stirring, for 1 to 2 minutes more, or until the shrimp are cooked through. Turn off the heat and stir in the parsley.

Spoon the cheesy grits into bowls and top with the shrimp. More cayenne can be used to dust the top if a spicier version is desired.

Serves 4

Crab Fritters with Avocado Salsa

Sweet crab and creamy avocado are always great together, and this tasty appetizer is no exception.

1½ cups frozen corn, thawed and drained, or lightly cooked fresh corn
2½ oz plain flour
2 eggs, beaten
10½ oz fresh or canned white crabmeat
1 small bunch fresh parsley, chopped
3 to 4 tbsps olive oil
Salt and pepper
Lime wedges, to serve

For the avocado salsa...
1 small red onion, finely chopped
1 red pepper
1 yellow pepper
1 avocado
1 mango
4 tomatoes
Juice and finely grated zest of 2 limes
1 large bunch fresh cilantro, chopped

First make the salsa. Put the onion in a bowl. Remove the stalks and seeds from the peppers, and cut the flesh into ½ inch dice. Add to the onion. Peel the avocado and mango, remove the stones and cut the flesh into ½ inch dice. Add to the bowl. Chop the tomatoes into ½ inch dice and add to the other ingredients. Stir in the lime juice and zest and cilantro. Season to taste with salt and pepper.

Put the sweetcorn kernels, flour and eggs in a separate bowl and stir until well mixed. Lightly fold in the crabmeat and parsley, and season to taste with salt and pepper.

Heat the oil in a large frying pan on the stove over a medium-high heat. Drop spoonfuls of the batter into the hot oil and cook in batches for 2 to 3 minutes on each side until crisp and golden. Remove and drain on kitchen paper. Serve immediately with the salsa and the lime wedges.

Serves 4

Oyster Po' Boys

Fried oysters are one of the most traditional fillings of this New Orleans classic. Once you choose your filling, you just have to decide if you want it "undressed" (plain) or "dressed" (with lettuce, tomatoes, and mayonnaise), as in this recipe.

Generous ¼ cup yellow cornmeal
⅓ cup all-purpose flour
Pinch of cayenne
24 fresh live oysters
Vegetable oil, for deep-frying
1 French baguette
Hot pepper sauce, to taste (optional)
2 dill pickles, sliced (optional)
Mayonnaise
4 tomatoes, sliced
Shredded iceberg lettuce
Salt and pepper

Put the cornmeal, flour, cayenne, and salt and pepper to taste into a plastic bag, hold closed, and shake to mix. Shuck the oysters, running an oyster knife under each oyster to loosen it from its shell. Pour off the liquor. Add the oysters to the bag and shake until well coated.

Heat at least 2 inches of oil in the largest skillet you have over high heat until the temperature reaches 350°F to 375°F, or until a cube of bread browns in 30 seconds. Add as many oysters as will fit without overcrowding and fry for 2 to 3 minutes until the coating is crisp and lightly browned. Remove the oysters from the oil with a slotted spoon and drain on paper towels. Reheat the oil, then cook the remaining oysters.

Cut the baguette in half, without cutting all the way through. Open the bread out like a book and use a spoon to scoop out the crumbs from the bottom half, leaving a border all around the edge.

Spread mayonnaise over the top and bottom halves. Lay the oysters all along the length. Sprinkle with hot pepper sauce to taste and dill pickles, if using. Dress with tomato slices all along the length, then add the shredded lettuce. Close the sandwich and cut into 4 equal portions and wrap in paper napkins to serve.

Serves 4

Classic Tuna Noodle Casserole

It's a mystery why the creamy and comforting tuna noodle casserole became synonymous with bad home cooking. There's nothing not to like about this great American retro classic.

12 oz package dry egg noodles
3 tbsps butter
½ yellow onion, finely diced
3 tbsps flour
3½ cups cold milk
1 (10 oz) can condensed cream of mushroom soup
1 tsp salt
¼ tsp freshly ground black pepper
2 (7 oz) cans tuna, well drained, crumbled
¾ cup frozen peas, thawed, drained
1 cup shredded cheddar cheese
½ cup shredded Monterey jack cheese
½ cup plain bread crumbs
2 tbsps olive oil

Pre-heat oven to 350°F.

Melt the butter in a medium saucepan, over medium-low heat, and sauté the onions for about 4 minutes, or until translucent. Turn up the heat to medium; add the flour, and cook, stirring, for another 2 minutes. While whisking vigorously, slowly pour in one cup of the cold milk.

When the mixture begins to simmer, add the rest of the milk, can of mushroom soup, salt, and pepper. Cook, stirring occasionally, until the sauce thickens, and comes to a simmer. Remove from heat, and reserve.

Cook noodles in boiling salted water, one minute less than the directions call for. Drain well, and add to a large mixing bowl. Add the sauce, tuna, peas and about two-thirds of the cheese. Mix with a spatula to combine.

Pour the mixture into a lightly oiled 9 x 13 casserole dish, and top with the rest of the cheese. Mix the breadcrumbs and olive oil together in a small bowl until combined. Sprinkle evenly over the casserole. Bake for 35 minutes, or until browned and bubbly.

Serves 6

Cornbread

This moist, crumbly version of America's oldest bread has a slight sweetness that makes it a perfect match for spicy foods. A warm, freshly cut wedge next to a steaming bowl of chili is a truly beautiful thing.

½ cup unsalted butter, melted
⅔ cup white granulated sugar
2 large eggs
1 cup buttermilk
½ tsp baking soda
½ tsp salt
1 cup all-purpose flour
1 cup yellow cornmeal
Extra butter to grease the pan

Pre-heat oven to 375°F.

In a large mixing bowl, whisk together the melted butter and sugar. Add the eggs; whisk until combined. Add the buttermilk and baking soda; whisk to combine. Add the flour, cornmeal, and salt. Using a spatula stir until just blended. Do not mix any longer than necessary.

Lightly grease a 10 inch cast iron skillet with butter. Pour in the batter and bake for about 35 minutes, or until a toothpick inserted in the center comes out clean. Let cool for at least 15 minutes before trying to cut.

Serves 6

Dinner Rolls

Making your own dinner rolls is surprisingly easy, and the taste of these soft rolls is far superior to anything from a store. Besides, few things can make your home smell as wonderful.

¼ cup warm water
1 packet (2¼ tsp) dry active yeast
1 cup milk
3 tbsps unsalted butter, room temperature
1 tbsp sugar
1 tbsp honey
¾ tsp salt
3 cups unbleached all-purpose white flour, plus more as needed
1 tsp vegetable oil

Pre-heat oven to 350°F.

Combine water and yeast in a large bowl. Whisk until dissolved, and set aside. Combine milk, butter, sugar, honey, and salt in another glass or plastic bowl. Microwave for one minute, or until milk is just warm. Set aside until butter is melted.

Add the flour to the bowl containing the water and yeast, followed by the milk mixture. Stir until a sticky dough forms. Turn dough out onto a well-floured work surface. Knead dough for about 6 minutes, adding enough flour, as needed to keep the dough from sticking to the surface, or your hands.

Stop when you have a smooth, soft, elastic ball of dough. Grease a large bowl with oil. Place the dough into the bowl and turn over a few times so the dough is lightly oiled. Cover the bowl with a clean towel and leave to rise in warm spot until it doubles in size, about 1½ hours.

Punch down the dough, and turn it out onto a lightly-floured surface. Shape into a square and cut into 16 equal-sized sections. Roll each piece into a ball. Line an 18 x 13 inch baking sheet with a silicon making mat. Place each ball, seam side down, about 2 inches apart on the baking sheet (4 rows with 4 rolls each).

Put a tsp of flour in a fine mesh sieve and tap to dust the top of each roll with a little flour. This is optional, but gives that classic dinner roll look. Set the pan in a warm spot and allow to rise for 40 minutes. It's okay if the rolls are slightly touching each other after they've risen.

Bake on the center rack for about 25 minutes, until golden brown. Remove and let cool on a rack for 20 minutes before serving.

Country Loaf

This old-fashioned loaf of rustic white bread is one of those recipes that will make you sad you don't bake more often.

1 packet (2¼ tsps) dry active yeast
¼ tsp sugar
1¼ cup warm water (105-110°F.)
3 cups unbleached white bread flour, divided
1 tsps salt
1 tsp vegetable oil
Cornmeal as needed

Pre-heat oven to 425°F.

Add the yeast, sugar, warm water, and 1½ cups of the flour to a large mixing bowl. Stir together until smooth, cover with a towel and leave in a warm spot (like an oven with the light on) for 2 hours.

Add 1 more cup of flour, and the salt, and stir to form a sticky dough. Turn dough out on a well-floured work surface. Knead dough for about 10 minutes, adding the last ½ cup of flour, but only as needed to keep the dough from sticking to the surface, or your hands. You want a very soft, supple, elastic dough, so use the flour very sparingly.

Grease a large bowl with vegetable oil. Form the dough into a ball, and place into the bowl; turn over a few times so the dough is lightly oiled. Cover the bowl with a towel and leave to rise in warm spot until it doubles in size, about 2 hours.

Prep a sheet pan by generously sprinkling with cornmeal. Punch down the dough, and turn it out onto a lightly-floured surface. Shape into an oval loaf and place on the baking sheet, seam side down.

Dust the top of the loaf lightly with flour and cover with a light, dry towel. Allow to rise for 1 hour in a warm spot.

Place a cake pan, half-filled with water on the bottom rack of the oven. When the oven is hot, remove the towel, and bake the bread on the middle rack for 45 minutes or until browned. Allow to cool completely on a rack before slicing.

Pizza Dough

This is the recipe your friendly neighborhood pizzeria does not want you to try.

1 package (2¼ tsps) dry active yeast
1 tsp honey
1 cup warm water (110°F.)
1 tsp salt
1½ tbsp olive oil
About 3 cups all-purpose flour

Dissolve yeast and honey in ¼ cup of warm water in a mixing bowl. Set stand 10 minutes. Add another ¾ cup of warm water, salt, olive oil, and 2½ cups of flour. Stir together to form a soft sticky dough.

Turn dough out onto a very well-floured work surface. Knead dough for about 5 minutes, adding just enough additional flour to keep the dough from sticking to the surface, or your hands. You want to end up with a fairly soft, elastic, and slightly sticky dough.

Lightly grease a large bowl with oil. Place the dough into the bowl and turn over a few times so the dough is lightly oiled. Cover the bowl with a clean towel and leave to rise in warm spot (like an oven with the light on), until it doubles in size, about 1 hour 15 minutes.

Turn dough out onto a lightly-floured surface, and press flat with your hands to deflate. Divide the dough into 4 equal-sized balls. Knead each ball briefly to form a smooth surface (using both hands, the dough ball can be stretched from the top down, and any seams tucked under the bottom of the ball).

Space each dough ball about 8 inches apart on a lightly-floured surface, dust the tops very lightly with flour, and cover with a clean towel; let rest for 30 minutes. At this point, the dough can be rolled out and used to make pizza, or wrapped in plastic and kept refrigerated for several days.

Makes 4 small pizzas

To make the pizza: Each ball of dough can be rolled out into an 8 to10-inch round pizza. If using a pizza stone, follow manufacturers directions.

Otherwise, preheat oven to 500°F. Dust a heavy-duty baking sheet with a circle of cornmeal just slightly larger than the pizza. Place the pizza on the pan and shake back and forth to make sure the dough is not sticking. Top sparingly with sauce, cheese, and toppings. The best pizzas are not weighed down with too much "stuff."

Place the pan directly on the bottom surface of the oven (for electric, on the lowest possible rack) for 5 minutes. This will help form a crisp bottom crust. After 5 minutes move the pan to the middle rack and cook for 3 to 5 minutes more, or until the bottom is browned and crisp, and the cheese is bubbling.

Buttermilk Biscuits

Making buttermilk biscuits would be the first event in any American food decathlon. Anyone can make them, but to get great biscuits it helps to have a gentle and intuitive disposition. Use a light touch because over-mixing will toughen the dough.

2 cups all-purpose flour
2 tsps baking powder
¼ tsp baking soda
1 tsp salt
7 tbsps unsalted butter, cut into thin slices, chilled in freezer
¾ cup cold buttermilk

Pre-heat oven to 425°F.

In a mixing bowl, whisk together the dry ingredients to thoroughly combine. Cut in the ice cold butter slices using a wire pastry blender, until the mixture has the texture of coarse crumbs.

Make a well in the center and pour in the cold buttermilk. Stir the dry ingredients into the buttermilk with a fork until a loose, sticky dough is formed. Stop as soon as the mixture comes together. Form into a ball and turn the dough out onto a floured work surface.

With floured hands, pat the dough into a rectangle (about 8 x 4 inch-thick). Fold dough in thirds (like folding a letter-sized piece of paper). Repeat this process twice more.

On a lightly-floured surface, roll or pat the dough out about ½ inch thick. Cut with a round biscuit cutter, and place on a parchment or silicon mat-lined baking sheet, a few inches apart. You can gather up any extra dough after cutting, and repeat to get a few more biscuits, although the texture may suffer from the extra working.

Make a slight depression in the center of each biscuit with your thumb (to help them rise evenly). Brush the tops lightly with buttermilk. Bake for about 15 minutes, or until risen and golden brown. Cool on a rack for 10 minutes before serving.

Makes 12-14

BREADS, BREAKFASTS & BRUNCH • BUTTERMILK BISCUITS

Banana Nut Bread

Next time those bananas are looking a little past their prime, remember this great nutty loaf.

2 cups all-purpose flour
1 tsp salt
1 tsp baking powder
1 tsp baking soda
½ cup unsalted butter, softened
1 cup white granulated sugar
2 large eggs
1½ cups mashed banana
(usually 3 bananas is perfect)
1 cup chopped walnuts
2 tbsps milk

Pre-heat oven to 325°F.

Whisk together the flour, salt, baking powder, and baking soda in a mixing bowl for a minute; reserve until needed.

Cream the butter and sugar together until light and fluffy. Beat in the eggs one at a time, mixing thoroughly before adding the next. Mix in the bananas, walnuts, and milk until combined. Add the flour mixture, stirring just until combined.

Pour batter into a buttered and lightly-floured 9 x 5 inch loaf pan. Bake for about 1 hour and 10 minutes, or until a toothpick inserted in the center comes out clean. Let cool 20 minutes before removing from the pan.

Serves 6

Hush Puppies

Few pan-fried catfish dinners in the South are served without a portion of these golden, deep-fried cornmeal dumplings on the side. Traditionally, they are cooked in the pan that the catfish was fried in, using the same fat for extra flavor.

1¾ cups yellow cornmeal
½ cup all-purpose flour, sifted
1 small onion, finely chopped
1 tbsp granulated white sugar
2 tsps baking powder
½ tsp salt
¾ cup milk
1 egg, beaten
Vegetable oil for deep-frying

Makes 36

Stir the cornmeal, flour, onion, sugar, baking powder, and salt together in a bowl and make a well in the center.

Beat the milk and egg together in a pitcher, then pour into the dry ingredients and stir until a thick batter forms.

Heat at least 2 inches of oil in a deep skillet or pan over high heat until the temperature reaches 350°F to 375°F, or until a cube of bread browns in 30 seconds.

Drop in as many tspfuls of the batter as will fit without overcrowding the skillet and cook, stirring constantly, until the Hush Puppies puff up and turn golden.

Remove the Hush Puppies from the oil with a slotted spoon and drain on paper towels. Reheat the oil, if necessary, and cook the remaining batter. Serve hot.

Cheese Blintzes with Strawberry Sauce

Blintzes are a wonderful special occasion breakfast or brunch treat. Eastern European immigrants brought these wonderful cheese filled crepes to New York City, and we're all better for it.

For the crepes...
1 cup whole milk
¼ cup cold water
2 large eggs
1 cup all-purpose flour
⅛ tsp salt
1 tbsp sugar
3 tbsps vegetable oil
Vegetable oil spray for cooking the crepes

For the filling...
1 ½ cups ricotta cheese
4 ounces cream cheese
3 tablespoons powdered sugar
1 teaspoon freshly grated lemon zest
1 large egg

For the sauce...
¾ cup strawberry preserves,
or any other fruit jam or jelly
¼ cup water

3 tbsps unsalted butter, for frying blintzes

Pre-heat oven to 400°F.

For the crepes: Pour the milk, water, eggs, flour, salt, sugar, and vegetable oil in a blender. Blend the batter until it is very smooth. Refrigerate for 1 to 2 hours before making crepes.

For the filling: Combine the ricotta cheese, cream cheese, powdered sugar, lemon zest, and egg in a food processor and blend until smooth. Refrigerate until needed.

To make the sauce: Add the strawberry preserves and water to a small saucepan and place over medium heat. Bring to a simmer, stirring, and turn off. Sauce may be strained if desired. Reserve until needed.

To cook the crepes: Place an 8 inch non-stick skillet over medium heat. Spray pan lightly with vegetable oil. Pour in ¼ cup of batter into the center of the pan and tilt it around so the batter covers the bottom evenly. Cook for about 1 minute, or until the crepe batter is set, then flip with a spatula and cook the other side for 30 seconds. Transfer the cooked crepes to a plate, and continue until the batter is gone. This should make about 8 to 10 crepes.

To make the blintzes: Spoon about 2 tbsp of the cheese filling into the center bottom third of a crepe. Fold the bottom up over the filling, fold in the sides, and roll to make a neat rectangular package (as you would a small burrito).

When the blintzes are filled and rolled, melt the butter in a non-stick skillet over medium heat. Brown the blintzes lightly on each side, starting with the seal side down. Transfer them to a lightly buttered baking dish.

Bake in oven for 15 minutes. Let rest for 5 minutes before serving with the fruit sauce. If you want them to look "fancier," dust with powdered sugar, but I think these are too beautiful to cover up with anything.

Makes 8-10

BREADS, BREAKFASTS & BRUNCH • CHEESE BLINTZES WITH STRAWBERRY SAUCE

Corned Beef Hash

To say that fresh, crusty homemade corned beef hash is superior to that pink paste from the can may be the biggest culinary understatement of all time.

2 tbsps butter
1 tbsp vegetable oil
1½ lbs cooked corned beef, cut in small cubes
½ cup diced onions
1½ lbs white potatoes, peeled, cut in small cubes
Salt and fresh ground black pepper to taste
¼ tsp paprika
¼ tsp garlic powder
¼ cup diced green bell pepper, or jalapeño
if a spicier version is desired
2 tbsps prepared roasted tomato salsa
1 tbsp freshly sliced chives

Add the butter, oil, corned beef, and onions to a large, cold, non-stick or well-seasoned cast iron skillet. Turn heat to medium-low and cook, stirring occasionally, while you prepare the potatoes.

In a saucepan, boil the potatoes in salted water for about 5 to 7 minutes (depending on the size), until partially cooked, but still very firm. Drain very well and add to the skillet along with the rest of the ingredients.

Mix together thoroughly with the hot corned beef mixture, and press down slightly with a spatula to flatten. Turn up the heat to medium. Every 10 minutes or so, turn the mixture over with a spatula to bring the crusty bottom, up to the top. Do this several times until the mixture is well-browned. Take your time – the only real secret to great corned beef hash is to make sure it cooks long enough, so the potatoes are crisp-edged, and the cubes of meat get nicely caramelized.

Taste for salt and pepper, and adjust if necessary. Transfer to plates, and top with poached eggs. Garnish with freshly chopped chives.

Potato Pancakes with Smoked Salmon & Dill Sour Cream

The secret to great potato pancakes is to make sure you squeeze out all the water before mixing. This will give you beautifully browned, crispy cakes. By the way, if you're out of smoked salmon, these are wonderful with applesauce.

2¼ lbs Russet potatoes, peeled
½ yellow onion, peeled
2 large eggs
3 tbsps all-purpose flour
1 tsp salt
½ tsp freshly ground black pepper
Pinch of cayenne
Vegetable oil, as needed
3 to 4 oz thinly sliced smoked salmon
4 tbsps sour cream
¼ cup fresh dill, chopped

Using a cheese grater, shred the potatoes, and quickly transfer into a large bowl of cold water. Grate the onion and add to bowl. Let sit for 20 minutes. Add the eggs, flour, salt, pepper, and cayenne to another large mixing bowl, and whisk until smooth; reserve.

Drain the potato mixture into a colander, pressing down to squeeze out as much water as possible. Line a baking sheet with several layers of paper towels. Take a handful of the potato mixture from the colander, and squeeze as hard as possible to extract even more water. Place the "dry" potatoes on the paper towels.

Repeat until all the potato mixture has been squeezed dry. Spread the potatoes evenly on the baking sheet and press down with some dry paper towels. Remove the paper towels and transfer the potato mixture to the bowl with the egg mixture. Use a spatula to combine thoroughly.

Pour about ¼ inch of vegetable oil into a large, heavy skillet (preferably non-stick). Place over medium-high heat, and when the oil is hot (the surface will begin to shimmer), spoon about ⅓ cup of the potato mixture into the pan, shape into a round, and flatten to about ½ inch thick. Turn down the heat to medium, and fry the potato pancakes for about 5 minutes per side, or until browned and crispy.

Remember, the potatoes are raw, so be sure they cook through. There is nothing worse than raw potatoes! You can probably fry 4 potato pancakes at a time. Drain on paper towels and hold in a warm oven until they're all done (or use 2 pans).

To serve, top with the sliced smoked salmon, a dollop of sour cream, the fresh dill, and a few grinds of black pepper.

Makes 8

Baked Spinach & Feta Omelet

You could use frozen, but with large bags of fresh, pre-washed and picked spinach so readily available in stores, why would you?

1 lb fresh spinach leaves, washed
1 tbsp butter
6 slices bacon, cut in ¼ inch pieces
½ onion, diced
12 eggs, beaten
Salt and freshly ground black pepper to taste
Pinch of cayenne
3 oz feta cheese, crumbled

Pre-heat oven to 350°F.

Put a large stockpot over high heat. Add the butter, and as soon as it melts, dump in all the spinach and cover the pot quickly. Leave for one minute, uncover, and continue cooking, stirring the spinach with a long wooden spoon, until just wilted. Transfer to a colander to drain. When the spinach is cool enough to handle, squeeze as much liquid out as possible, and roughly chop. Reserve until needed.

In a 10 to 12 inch ovenproof skillet, cook the bacon over medium heat until almost crisp, add the onions and a pinch of salt, and continue cooking until the onions are translucent, about 6 to 7 minutes. Any excess bacon fat can be removed at this point.

Stir in the spinach. Season with salt, freshly ground black pepper, and cayenne to taste. When the spinach is heated through, add the eggs and stir with a spatula to combine thoroughly. Turn off the heat, and top with the crumbled feta cheese. Use the spatula to press the cheese down into the egg slightly.

Bake for 10 minutes, then finish under the broiler for about 3 minutes, or until the eggs are just set, and the top is lightly browned. Let rest for 5 to 10 minutes before slicing and serving.

Serves 6

New Orleans Style French Toast

This recipe was born as a deliciously decadent solution for what to do with stale loaves!

5 large eggs
1 cup milk
½ cup cream
Pinch of salt
1 tbsp sugar
2 tsps vanilla
½ tsp cinnamon
⅛ tsp allspice
12 thick slices day-old French bread
(use a regular sized loaf, not the skinny
baguette type)
6 tbsps butter, plus more as needed

Pre-heat oven to 375°F.

In a large mixing bowl, whisk together the eggs, milk, cream, salt, sugar, vanilla, cinnamon, and allspice. Soak the bread slices in the custard mixture for at least 20 minutes, or until completely saturated.

In a large non-stick skillet, lightly brown the slices in batches, in a few tbsps of butter over medium heat; about 2 minutes per side. Don't cook too dark, as additional browning will occur in the oven.

Transfer to lightly buttered, foil-lined sheet pans, and bake for 10 minutes. After 10 minutes, remove, and turn each slice over. Put back in the oven for another 10 to 15 minutes, or until browned and the bread springs back slightly when tested with a finger.

Serve immediately.

Serves 4-6

Blueberry Pancakes

When it's summer in Maine, the state's blueberries feature at every meal, starting with breakfast, when they flavor muffins and pancakes. For a complete New England breakfast, serve these with Vermont maple syrup.

1 cup all-purpose flour
2 tbsps granulated white sugar
2 tsps baking powder
½ tsp salt
1 cup buttermilk
3 tbsps butter, melted
1 large egg
5 oz blueberries, rinsed and patted dry

To serve...
Butter
Warm maple syrup

Pre-heat oven to 275°F.

Sift the flour, sugar, baking powder, and salt together into a large bowl and make a well in the center.

Beat the buttermilk, butter, and egg together in a separate small bowl, then pour the mixture into the well in the dry ingredients. Beat the dry ingredients into the liquid, gradually drawing them in from the side, until a smooth batter forms. Gently stir in the blueberries.

Heat a large skillet over medium-high heat until a splash of water dances on the surface. Use a pastry brush or crumpled piece of paper towel and the oil to lightly grease the base of the skillet.

Use a ladle to drop about 4 tbsps of batter into the skillet and spread it out into a 4 inch round. Continue adding as many pancakes as will fit in your skillet. Leave the pancakes to cook until small bubbles appear on the surface, then flip them over and cook for a further 1 to 2 minutes until the bottoms are golden brown.

Transfer the pancakes to a warmed plate and keep warm in the oven while you cook the remaining batter, lightly greasing the skillet as before. Serve with a pat of butter on top of each pancake and warm maple syrup for pouring over.

Makes 10-12

Eggs Benedict

This dish is the undisputed king of brunch entrees. The trick here is poaching the eggs ahead so you can assemble all the plates at the same time.

12 very fresh large eggs
12 slices Canadian bacon
6 English muffins
Butter as needed

For the hollandaise...
1 cup (2 sticks) unsalted butter
5 large egg yolks
2 tbsps fresh lemon juice
Cayenne to taste
Salt to taste

To prep the eggs: Working in small batches, poach eggs in a saucepan of very gently simmering salted water to which a tbsp of white vinegar has been added. As they're done carefully set them into a bowl of cool water. Reserve until needed.

To make the hollandaise: Melt the butter in a small saucepan, and reserve over very low heat until needed. Add the egg yolks and lemon juice to a medium stainless steel bowl. Place over a saucepan with 2 inches of gently simmering water (note: the bowl should not be touching the water). Whisk constantly until the mixture thickens and is very warm to the touch.

Remove from the heat and very slowly drizzle in the hot melted butter, whisking constantly until it's all incorporated. The mixture can be thinned with a tbsp of hot water if desired. Whisk in the cayenne and salt to taste. Cover with foil and keep in a warm spot until needed.

To complete the plates: Bring a large deep skillet filled with 3 inches of salted water to a simmer. Place the English muffin halves on a baking sheet and toast under the broiler until golden, then brush with butter. Place one slice of Canadian bacon on each muffin half. Turn off the heat and keep the pan in the warm oven until the eggs are reheated.

Carefully transfer the poached eggs into the simmer water for 2 minutes until heated through but still soft. Remove eggs with a slotted spoon, and place one on each muffin half. Spoon over the warm hollandaise and serve immediately.

Serves 6

BREADS, BREAKFASTS & BRUNCH • EGGS BENEDICT

Sausage Mushroom Breakfast Casserole

This hearty breakfast casserole is great hot, but can also be served at room temperature. Be sure to check the fridge before making this, since it's a great way to use up leftover produce. Hey, isn't that a bell pepper in the back of the vegetable drawer?

2 tbsps butter
1½ lbs potatoes, peeled,
cut into 1 inch chunks
1 lb sweet or hot Italian sausage (or sausage
of your choice), casing removed
1 bunch green onions, chopped
2 cups shredded cheddar cheese, divided
1 lb sliced button mushrooms
14 eggs, beaten
¼ cup milk
1½ tsp salt
½ tsp fresh ground black pepper
Dash of Tabasco, optional

Pre-heat oven to 300°F.

Boil the potatoes in salted water until just tender, and drain well. Grease a 13 x 9 inch baking dish with 1 tbsp of the butter, and add the potatoes. Top with half the cheese.

Brown the sausage in a skillet over medium heat, breaking it into small pieces with a spatula or wooden spoon as it cooks. When browned, add the green onions and cook for 2 minutes more. Use a slotted spoon to transfer the sausage and onions into the baking dish.

Pour off any excess grease from the pan, and add the butter and mushrooms. Add a pinch of salt and cook, stirring, over high heat until well-browned. Add mushrooms to the baking dish and distribute evenly.

Whisk together the eggs, milk, salt, freshly ground black pepper, and Tabasco in a mixing bowl. Pour over the sausage and mushrooms. Give the baking dish a jiggle or two, to make sure the eggs are distributed. Top with the rest of the cheese.

Bake for about 35 minutes, or until just set. If desired, place under a hot broiler for a minute or two to brown the top. Let rest at least 15 minutes before serving. May be served room temperature.

Serves 6-8

Red Velvet Cake

This is one of the few recipes left where it's completely acceptable, if not mandatory, to use food coloring. Some older recipes actually call for beets to give this southern staple its signature color. As delicious as a "beet-infused cake" sounds, we'll just stick with a natural red dye.

1 cup unsalted butter, plus extra for greasing
4 tbsp water
½ cup unsweetened cocoa
3 eggs
Generous 1 cup buttermilk
2 tsps vanilla extract
2 tbsps red food coloring
2½ cups all-purpose flour
½ cup cornstarch
1½ tsps baking powder
Scant 1½ cups granulated white sugar

For the frosting...
Generous 1 cup cream cheese
3 tbsps unsalted butter
3 tbsps granulated white sugar
1 tsp vanilla extract

Pre-heat oven to 375°F.

Grease 2 x 9 inch layer cake pans and line the bottoms with parchment paper.

Place the butter, water, and cocoa in a small saucepan and heat gently, without boiling, stirring until melted and smooth. Remove from the heat and let cool slightly.

Beat together the eggs, buttermilk, vanilla extract, and food coloring until frothy. Beat in the butter mixture. Sift together the flour, cornstarch, and baking powder, then stir quickly and evenly into the mixture with the granulated white sugar.

Divide the batter between the prepared pans and bake in the pre-heated oven for 25 to 30 minutes, or until risen and firm to the touch. Cool in the pans for 3 to 4 minutes, then turn out and finish cooling on a wire rack.

For the frosting, beat together all the ingredients until smooth. Use about half of the frosting to sandwich the cakes together, then spread the remainder over the top, swirling with a metal spatula.

Serves 12

Pound Cake with Orange Glaze

Perfect with a cup of tea or coffee, this simple pound cake is also great sitting under some fresh fruit.

9 oz (2 cups) all-purpose flour
1 tsp baking powder
¼ tsp baking soda
½ tsp salt
2 sticks (1 cup) unsalted butter
1¼ cups white sugar
1 tbsp grated lemon zest
1 tbsp grated orange zest
4 eggs
½ cup buttermilk
1 tsp vanilla extract

For the glaze...
1 cup powdered sugar
1½ tbsps fresh orange juice, or as needed
1 tbsp freshly grated orange zest

Pre-heat oven to 325°F.

Butter one loaf pan, and dust with flour. Set aside.

Sift together the flour, baking powder, baking soda, and salt in a mixing bowl. Set aside.

In a large mixing bowl, use an electric mixer to beat the butter, sugar, and zests until very light and creamy. Beat in the eggs, one at time, beating very thoroughly after each addition. Use a spatula to mix in flour alternately with the buttermilk, ending with flour. Scrape the batter into the prepared loaf pan.

Bake for 1 hour to 1 hour 15 minutes, or until a toothpick inserted in the center comes out clean. Remove and let rest for 15 minutes, then turn onto a cooling rack. Let cool 15 more minutes before glazing.

Stir together the orange glaze ingredients, adding enough orange juice to get a smooth spreadable consistency. Apply to the top of the warm cake. Let the pound cake cool completely before slicing.

Carrot Cake with Cream Cheese Frosting

If someone did a list of the greatest cake/frosting combinations of all time, this dense, moist carrot cake topped with cream cheese frosting has to be at the top.

2 cups all-purpose flour
1 tsp salt
2 tsps baking powder
1 tsp baking soda
2 tsps cinnamon
½ tsp ground ginger
2 cups sugar
1¼ cups vegetable oil
4 large eggs
¼ cup melted butter
2 cups raw grated carrots
1 can (8 oz) crushed pineapple, drained
½ cup chopped pecans
½ cup chopped walnuts

For the frosting...
½ cup unsalted butter, softened
8 oz cream cheese, softened
1 tbsp milk
1 tsp vanilla
1 lb powdered sugar

Pre-heat oven to 350°F.

Whisk together the flour, salt, baking powder, baking soda, cinnamon, and ginger in a mixing bowl for a minute or two; reserve until needed.

In another mixing bowl, combine the sugar, oil, and eggs. Whisk until thoroughly combined. Whisk in the melted butter. Use a spatula to stir in the carrots, pineapple, and nuts. Stir in the flour mixture in two additions.

Scrape the batter into a lightly greased 13 x 9 inch dish. Bake for about 40 minutes, or until the top springs back slightly when gently touched with your finger. Remove and allow to cool completely before frosting.

To make the frosting: Use an electric mixer to beat together the butter, cream cheese, milk, and vanilla until light and fluffy. Gradually beat in the powdered sugar to form a smooth frosting. Spread evenly over the cooled cake.

Serves 8

Chocolate Chip Cookies

A well-made chocolate chip is about as close to cookie perfection as you'll ever get.

2¼ cups all-purpose flour
1 tsp baking soda
1 tsp salt
1 cup butter, room temperature
¾ cup packed light brown sugar
¾ cup white granulated sugar
1 tsp vanilla extract
2 large eggs
2 cups dark or semi-sweet chocolate chips
1 cup chopped walnuts, optional

Pre-heat oven to 375°F.

Add the flour, baking soda and salt to a small mixing bowl. Whisk together briefly to combine. In another bowl, use an electric mixer to beat the butter, brown sugar, white granulated sugar, and vanilla extract until light and creamy.

Add eggs one at a time, beating thoroughly after each addition. Stir in the flour mixture until combined. Stir in the chocolate chips and nuts, if using. Drop the cookie dough by rounded tbsps on un-greased cookie sheets about 3 inches apart.

Bake for about 10 minutes, or until lightly browned around the edges. Let sit on the baking sheets for 2 minutes, and then remove to wire cooling racks.

Makes 30

Peanut Butter Cookies

You know that feeling when you're really craving something good, but can't decide what that something is? It's these melt-in-your-mouth peanut butter cookies.

1½ cups all-purpose flour
½ tsp baking powder
½ tsp salt
1 cup creamy peanut butter
½ cup butter, room temperature
1¼ tsps vanilla extract
½ cup brown sugar
½ cup white sugar
2 eggs

Pre-heat oven to 350°F.

Sift together the flour, baking powder, and salt in a mixing bowl; reserve. In a large mixing bowl, cream the peanut butter, butter, and vanilla together until smooth. Add the sugars, and cream for one more minute. Mix in the eggs one at a time. Mix in the flour, half at a time.

Wrap the dough in plastic wrap and refrigerate for at least 2 hours. Once chilled, roll or scoop the dough into 1½ inch balls, and place 3 inches apart on an ungreased or silicon-lined baking sheet.

Use a fork to flatten each ball by making a crisscross pattern. Bake for 15 minutes or until golden. Remove cookies from oven, and let cool on the baking sheet for 5 minutes. Transfer to a cooling rack with a spatula, and allow to cool to at least warm before enjoying.

Makes 12-15

Boston Cream Pie

Sure you can make one from scratch for this, but let's face it, the cake in this classic American dessert is nothing more than a chocolate and pastry cream delivery system.

1 (18.25 oz) package white or yellow cake mix, prepared according to directions

For the pastry cream...
1 cup whipping cream
1 cup whole milk
1 tbsp butter
7 tbsps sugar
2 tbsps cornstarch
3 large eggs
1½ tsps pure vanilla extract
Pinch of salt

For the chocolate topping (called a ganache)...
4 oz high-quality bittersweet chocolate, chopped
½ cup heavy cream
1 tsp butter

For the pastry cream: Combine the sugar, cornstarch, and eggs in a mixing bowl; whisk vigorously until the mixture is light and creamy, and thin ribbons form on the surface when the whisk is lifted out of the mixture; set aside.

Bring the cream, milk, and butter to a boil in a small saucepan over medium-high heat. Quickly whisk in the egg mixture, and boil, stirring constantly, for exactly one minute. The mixture should become very thick, very quickly. Remove from heat and strain into a clean bowl. Cover the surface with plastic wrap, and let cool at room temp for 20 minutes. Place in the fridge until completely cold; overnight is best. Before using, whisk in the vanilla, and season with a pinch of salt to taste.

Once your pastry cream is ready, and your cakes have been baked and completely cooled, you're ready to assemble. Since one mix makes 2 layer cakes, you have a decision to make regarding the cake-to-cream ratio.

You can place one layer down on a cake plate, top with the pastry cream and lay the other cake gently on top. Or, if you want less cake to get in the way of the cream filling and chocolate, you can just use one layer. If using one layer, take a long serrated knife and slice the cake through the center to make 2 thinner layers. Either way, you'll have two layers of cake sandwiching your vanilla pastry cream.

For the chocolate topping: Place the chopped chocolate in a small heatproof bowl and set aside. Bring the cream and butter to a simmer over medium-high heat, then quickly pour over the chocolate. Let sit undisturbed for 3 minutes, then gently whisk to combine.

The chocolate mixture will slowly thicken as it cools. When the mixture has thickened slightly, yet is still just thin enough to pour, spread evenly over the top of the cake. Start in the center and slowly work the chocolate toward the edges. Refrigerate until the chocolate has firmed up completely before slicing and serving.

Serves 6-8

Chocolate Walnut Fudge

Contrary to what you might have heard, chocolate fudge is not hard to make. This easy recipe produces rich, smooth fudge every time.

1½ cups white granulated sugar
1 (7 oz) jar marshmallow crème
⅔ cup evaporated milk
3 tbsps butter
¼ tsp salt
1½ cups milk chocolate chips
1½ cups semisweet chocolate chips
½ cup chopped walnuts, optional
1 tsp vanilla extract
2 tsps cocoa, optional

Line an 8 x 8 inch pan with foil, and set aside. Add the sugar, marshmallow crème, evaporated milk, butter, and salt to a large, heavy-bottomed saucepan; place over medium heat. Cook, stirring, until the mixture begins to boil. When it begins to boil, set a timer for exactly 6 minutes. Stir constantly until the timer rings.

Turn off heat, and pour in the chocolate chips. Stir until the chocolate is melted, then add the walnuts and vanilla. Pour into the pan, and spread evenly. Cover and refrigerate until firm. Cut into 36 squares, and dust with cocoa if desired.

Double Fudge Brownies

If you like dry, cake-like brownies, this recipe isn't for you.
These are moist, fudgy, azery chocolaty.

8 oz bittersweet baking chocolate, broken or chopped into small pieces
⅓ cup butter, sliced into pieces
1 cup white granulated sugar
¼ tsp salt
2 tbsps water
2 large eggs
1 tsp vanilla extract
¾ cup all-purpose flour
½ cup chopped walnuts (optional)

Pre-heat oven to 325°F.

Place the chocolate, butter, sugar, salt, and water in small saucepan over a very low flame. Heat, stirring often, until the chocolate and butter are melted.

Pour into a mixing bowl. Stir in the eggs, one at a time. Stir in the vanilla. Stir in the flour. Stir in the nuts, if using.

Pour into a lightly greased 8 inch-square baking dish.

Bake for 35 minutes. Cool completely before cutting into 9 squares.

Makes 9

Butterscotch Blondies

Bored with brownies? It's okay, it happens to everyone. When it does, what better alternative than moist and tender butterscotch blondies?

½ cup butter, melted
¾ cup packed brown sugar
¼ cup white granulated sugar
1 large egg plus 1 egg yolk, beaten together
1 tsp vanilla extract
½ tsp baking powder
⅛ tsp baking soda
¼ tsp salt
1 cup all-purpose flour
½ cup butterscotch chips
¼ cup milk chocolate chips
¼ cup chopped dry-roasted cashews

Pre-heat oven to 350°F.

Add the flour, baking soda, baking powder, and salt to a mixing bowl. Stir with a whisk to combine. Reserve.

In another large mixing bowl, whisk together the melted butter and sugars until combined. Add the eggs and vanilla, and stir to combine. Switch to a wooden spoon and stir in the flour mixture. Fold in the butterscotch chips, chocolate chips, and cashews.

With a spatula, scrape the batter into a lightly greased 8 x 8 inch pan or glass baking dish. Smooth to distribute evenly. Bake for about 35 minutes, or until the top is golden brown and a toothpick inserted in the center comes out clean.

Cool before cutting into 9 bars.

Makes 9

Cinnamon Swirl Sour Cream Bundt Cake

I didn't add the word "Coffee" to the title of this recipe because it was already too long, but make no mistake, this is a coffee cake. In fact, if you don't drink coffee, please start before attempting this moist, spicy cake.

2½ cups all-purpose flour
1 tsp baking powder
1 tsp baking soda
½ tsp salt
¾ cup (1½ sticks) unsalted butter
1½ cups white granulated sugar
3 large eggs
1 cup sour cream
1 tsp vanilla extract
½ cup chopped walnuts, optional

For the swirl...
1 tbsp ground cinnamon
3 tbsps brown sugar
2 tbsps white granulated sugar

For the glaze...
1 cup powdered sugar
About 1½ tbsps milk
1 tsp ground cinnamon, or to taste

Pre-heat oven to 350°F.

Whisk together the flour, baking powder, baking soda, and salt in a mixing bowl for a minute; reserve until needed.

Cream the butter and sugar together until light and fluffy. Beat in the eggs one at a time, mixing thoroughly before adding the next. Beat in the sour cream and vanilla until combined. Add the flour mixture, stirring just until combined. Stir in the walnuts.

Butter a 10 inch bundt pan, and lightly dust with flour. Pour half the batter into the pan and spread evenly. Mix the ingredients for the swirl in a small bowl. Sprinkle evenly around the center of the batter. Cover with the rest of the batter.

Bake for 50 minutes, or until a toothpick inserted in the center comes out clean. Let cool 20 minutes before removing from the pan.

For the glaze: Add the powdered sugar to a small mixing bowl, stir in enough milk to create a thick, but pourable glaze. Stir in the cinnamon to taste. Drizzle over the top of the cake. Once the icing is set, slice and serve with lots of hot coffee.

Lemon Poppy Seed Muffins

Remember that day you were so busy you missed breakfast, and had to settle for grabbing a lemon poppy seed muffin on the way out? That was a pretty good morning.

2 cups all-purpose flour
½ tsp salt
1½ tsps baking powder
¼ tsp baking soda
1 stick (½ cup) unsalted butter, softened
1 cup white granulated sugar
Finely grated zest from 2 lemons
2 large eggs
2 tbsps lemon juice
1 cup sour cream
2 tbsps poppy seeds

For the glaze...
1 tbsp lemon juice
3 tbsps powdered sugar

Pre-heat oven to 350°F.

Whisk together the flour, salt, baking powder, and baking soda in a bowl, and reserve until needed.

In a mixing bowl, beat the butter, sugar, and lemon zest, until light and creamy. Beat in the eggs one at a time, mixing thoroughly before adding the next. Stir in a third of the flour mixture until just combined. Stir in the lemon juice, and half of the sour cream until combined.

Add half of the remaining flour mixture, and stir until combined. Stir in the remaining sour cream. Stir in the rest of the flour mixture, and then the poppy seeds.

Line a 12 inch muffin tin with paper baking cups. Fill each to the top with batter. Bake about 30 minutes, or until golden brown and a toothpick inserted in the center comes out clean. While the muffins are baking, mix the lemon juice and powdered sugar together to form a thin glaze.

Remove the muffins from the oven when ready, and allow to cool for 5 minutes. Brush the lemon glaze evenly over the top of each muffin. This is not intended to be a frosting, but just a very light glaze to give the tops a little shine and extra kiss of lemon flavor.

When cool enough to handle, remove muffins from the tins and cool completely on a rack before serving.

Makes 12

Blueberry Muffins

The sour cream gives these blueberry muffins a nice richness, and keeps them moist and tender.

3 cups all-purpose flour
¾ tsp salt
1 tbsp baking powder
½ tsp baking soda
1 cup white granulated sugar
1 (½ cup) stick butter, softened
finely grated zest from one lemon
2 tbsps vegetable oil
2 large eggs
1 cup sour cream
½ cup milk
½ tsp lemon extract, optional
2 cups fresh blueberries

Pre-heat oven to 375°F.

Sift together the flour, salt, baking powder, and baking soda into a bowl; reserve.

In a large mixing bowl, beat the sugar, butter, lemon zest, and vegetable oil until light and creamy. Beat in the eggs one at a time. Whisk in the sour cream, milk, and lemon extract.

Add half the dry ingredients, and stir until just barely combined. Add the remaining dry ingredients, along with the blueberries, and fold with a spatula until just combined.

Line your muffin tins with paper baking cups. Fill each to the top with batter. Bake 30 minutes to a beautiful golden brown. When cool enough to handle, remove muffins from the tins and serve.

Serves 16

Whoopie Pies

You have to love any recipe whose name comes from the joyous exclamation they cause. "Whoopie!" indeed.

2 cups all-purpose flour
3 tbsps unsweetened cocoa powder
½ tsp baking soda
¼ tsp salt
1 stick (½ cup) unsalted butter, softened
1 cup packed brown sugar
1 large egg
1¼ tsps vanilla
½ cup buttermilk

For the filling...
4 oz softened cream cheese
1 (7 oz) jar marshmallow creme

Pre-heat oven to 375°F.

Add the flour, cocoa powder, baking soda and salt to a mixing bowl. Stir the mixture enthusiastically with a whisk to combine and aerate. Reserve until needed.

Add the butter and brown sugar to a large mixing bowl, and beat with an electric mixer until light and fluffy. Beat in the egg and vanilla until thoroughly combined.

Add a third of the flour mixture; stir until combined. Add half the buttermilk; stir until combined. Add half the remaining flour; stir until combined. Add the remaining buttermilk, stir in, and finally mix in the last of the flour.

Line two heavy-duty baking sheets with silicon baking mats or parchment paper.

Spoon the batter on the baking sheets, forming rounds about ½ inch high and 3 inches wide. You should fit about 8 per pan. As long as the batter is spooned on about ½ inch thick, you can really make these as small or large as you like. The most important thing is they all remain the same size, so they bake evenly.

Bake for 12 to 14 minutes, or until the tops look cooked, and are slightly firm to the touch (be gentle). Remove and let rest for 15 minutes on the baking sheets. Remove to racks and let cool completely before filling.

In a mixing bowl beat the cream cheese until light and fluffy. Use a spatula to fold in the marshmallow creme. Spread a couple spoons of filling on the flat side of one of the cakes, and top with another to form a sandwich.

Makes 8-10

Apple Pie

This recipe is dedicated to everyone who realizes that, "As American as apple piepie", is much more than just a saying.

For the crust...
12 oz flour (about 2½ cups)
2 stickst (1 cup) ice cold butter,
cut into ½ inch pieces
½ tsp salt
7 tbsps ice water
1 tbsp cider vinegar

For the filling...
6 baking apples
½ lemon, juiced
1 cup white sugar
3 tbsps cornstarch
Pinch of nutmeg
½ tsp cinnamon
2 tbsps butter

1 beaten egg to glaze the crust

For the crust: Add the flour into the bowl of a food processor, with the regular blade attached. Add the butter and salt. Pulse on and off until the mixture resembles coarse crumbs.

Mix the water and vinegar together. Pour half into the processor, and pulse on and off several times. Add the rest of the mixture, and again pulse on and off several times, until the dough gets crumbly, and just starts to clump together. Do not over-mix.

Transfer the dough onto a work surface, and shape the dough into a ball with your hands. Cut in half and shape each half into a disc about 5 inches wide. Wrap in plastic and chill in the refrigerator for 30 minutes.

Pre-heat oven to 375°F.

For the filling: Peel, core, and slice the apples into thin slices. Toss the apple slices with the lemon juice in a large mixing bowl. Add the rest of the filling ingredients, except the butter, and mix until well combined.

Place a sheet pan on the bottom of the oven in case the juices bubble out, which they often do.

Roll half the dough on a lightly floured surface to form the bottom crust. It should be rolled large enough to cover a 9 inch pie dish or pan with a few inches to spare all around. Place and press into the pan.

Pour the apple mixture into the bottom crust, packing firmly and evenly. Dot the top of the apples with the butter. Brush the exposed dough lightly with the beaten egg. Roll out the second half of the dough and cover the mounded apples.

Press the two pieces of dough together with your fingers. Pinch the edges so that both crusts are sealed all the way around the pan. Some like to go around the edge with a fork to make a design, and help seal the dough, while others like to "crimp" the edge using their fingers to make the traditional scalloped edge. As you can see from the photo, I'm a crimper.

Cut a few slashes in the top crust so the steam can escape. Brush the top crust with the beaten egg. Bake for 1 to 1½ hours (depending on the apples used), until the crust is nicely browned, and the apples are tender when tested with a small knife through the slits on the top. If the crust begins to brown too quickly, tent with foil. Let cool completely before serving.

Vanilla Ice Cream With Chocolate Sauce

Simply put; there is nothing like homemade ice cream.

For the ice cream...
4 large egg yolks
1 cup white granulated sugar
1 cup whole milk
2 cups whipping cream
1 whole vanilla bean

For the sauce...
½ cup heavy cream
4 oz dark chocolate,
broken into small pieces
2 tbsps orange liqueur

For the ice cream: Add egg yolks, sugar, milk, and cream to a heavy-bottomed saucepan. Whisk thoroughly to combine.

Split the vanilla bean lengthwise and scrape out the seeds with the back of the knife. Add the pod and the seeds to the mixture. Place over medium-low heat.

Cook, stirring constantly with a silicon spatula, until the mixture reaches a temperature of 175°F. This will be just below a simmer, but best to use a thermometer. Do not allow the mixture to boil.

Remove from heat and place saucepan over a bowl of ice water to cool, stirring occasionally. Remove the vanilla bean and pour the cooled mixture into a container with a tight-fitting lid. Cover and refrigerate mixture at least 4 hours, or overnight for best results.

Freeze mixture in an ice cream maker according to the manufacturer's instructions. Transfer the mixture back into the container, cover and allow to harden in the freezer for a couple hours before serving.

For the sauce: Bring the cream gently to a boil in a small heavy-bottomed pan over low heat. Remove the pan from the heat, add the broken chocolate, and stir until smooth.

Stir in the liqueur and serve immediately, or keep the sauce warm until required.

Makes 1 quart

Sweet Potato Pie

And you thought sweet potatoes were just something you picked at once a year around the Thanksgiving table.

For the pie dough...
1¼ cups all-purpose flour, plus extra for dusting
½ tsp salt
¼ tsp granulated white sugar
1½ tbsps butter, diced
3 tbsps vegetable shortening, diced
2 to 2½ tbsps ice-cold water

For the filling...
1 lb 2 oz orange-fleshed
sweet potatoes, scrubbed
3 extra-large eggs, beaten
½ cup packed brown sugar
1½ cups canned evaporated milk
3 tbsps butter, melted
2 tsps vanilla extract
1 tsp ground cinnamon
1 tsp ground nutmeg or freshly grated nutmeg
½ tsp salt
Freshly whipped cream, to serve

Pre-heat oven to 425°F.

To make the pie dough, sift the flour, salt, and sugar into a bowl. Add the butter and vegetable shortening to the bowl and rub in with the fingertips until fine crumbs form. Sprinkle over 2 tbsps of the water and mix with a fork until a soft dough forms. Add ½ tbsp of water if the dough is too dry. Wrap in plastic wrap and chill for at least 1 hour.

Meanwhile, bring a large pan of water to a boil over high heat. Add the sweet potatoes and cook for 15 minutes. Drain, then cool them under cold running water. When cool, peel, then mash. Put the sweet potatoes into a separate bowl and beat in the eggs and sugar until very smooth. Beat in the remaining ingredients, except the whipped cream, then set aside until required.

Roll out the dough on a lightly floured counter into a thin 11 inch circle and use to line a 9 inch pie plate, about 1½ inches high. Trim off the excess dough and press the floured tines of a fork around the edge.

Prick the base of the pastry shell all over with the fork and place crumpled kitchen foil in the center. Bake in the oven for 12 minutes, or until lightly golden.

Remove the pastry shell from the oven, take out the foil, pour the filling into the shell, and return to the oven for an additional 10 minutes. Reduce the oven temperature to 325°F and bake for a further 35 minutes, or until a knife inserted into the center comes out clean.

Let cool on a cooling rack. Serve warm or at room temperature with whipped cream.

Serves 8-10

New York Cheesecake with Fruit Sauce

Apples are okay, but this decadent dessert begs the question, why isn't New York called "The Big Cheesecake"?

½ cup butter
1¾ cups finely crushed grahams crackers
1 tbsp granulated white sugar
2 lbs cream cheese
1¼ cups granulated white sugar
2 tbsps all purpose flour
1 tsp vanilla extract
Finely grated zest of 1 orange
Finely grated zest of 1 lemon
3 eggs
2 egg yolks
1¼ cups heavy cream

For the sauce...
8 oz berries, such as
blackberries or raspberries
2 tbsps water
2 to 3 tbsps granulated white sugar
2 tbsps fruit liqueur, such as crème de cassis
or crème de framboise

Pre-heat the oven to 350°F.

Place a small saucepan over low heat, melt the butter and remove from heat. Stir in crushed crackers and the 1 tbsp sugar. Mix. Press the cracker mixture into bottom of a 9 inch cake pan. Place in an oven and bake for 10 minutes. Remove and cool.

Increase oven temperature to 400°F.

With an electric food mixer beat cream cheese until creamy and gradually add sugar and flour and beat until smooth. Beat in the vanilla extract, orange and lemon zest, then one at a time beat in the eggs and egg yolks. Finally beat in the cream. The mixture should be light and whippy.

Grease the sides of the cake pan and pour in the filling. Transfer to the pre-heated oven and bake for 15 minutes. Reduce heat to 200°F. and bake for an additional 30 minutes. Turn the oven off and leave to cool for 2 hours. Cover and refrigerate overnight.

For the sauce: Put all the ingredients into a small, heavy-bottomed pan and heat gently, until the sugar has dissolved and the fruit juices run. Process to a paste in a food processor, then push through a non-metallic strainer into a serving bowl to remove the seeds. Add more sugar if necessary and serve warm or cold.

Serves 8-10

Lemon Meringue Pie

This classic American pie has been a great favorite since the 1960s, when it was available in many restaurants. It has three distinct parts: the crisp pastry base; the tangy, smooth lemon center; and the meringue topping, crispy on the outside yet oozing and marshmallowy inside.

Salted/unsalted butter, for greasing
9 oz ready-made unsweetened pie dough, thawed if frozen
All-purpose flour, for dusting
3 tbsps cornstarch
½ cup granulated white sugar
Grated rind of 3 lemons
1¼ cups cold water
⅔ cup lemon juice
3 egg yolks
½ stick unsalted butter, diced

For the meringue...
3 egg whites
1 cup granulated white sugar
1 tsp golden granulated sugar

Pre-heat oven to 400°F.

Grease a 10 inch fluted flan pan with butter. Roll out the pastry on a lightly-floured counter into a circle 2 inches larger than the flan pan. Ease the pastry into the pan without stretching and press down lightly into the corners and trim the edge. Prick the base with a fork and chill, uncovered, in the refrigerator for 20 to 30 minutes.

Line the pastry shell with parchment paper and fill with dried beans. Bake on a pre-heated baking sheet for 15 minutes. Remove the beans and paper and return to the oven for 10 minutes, or until the pastry is dry and just colored. Remove from the oven and reduce the temperature to 300°F.

Put the cornstarch, granulated white sugar, and lemon rind in a pan. Pour in a little of the water and blend to a smooth paste. Gradually add the remaining water and the lemon juice. Bring the mixture to a boil over medium heat, stirring constantly. Simmer gently for 1 minute, or until smooth and glossy. Remove from the heat and beat in the egg yolks, one at a time, then beat in the butter. Put the pan in a bowl of cold water to cool the filling. When cool, spoon into the pastry shell.

For the meringue, whisk the egg whites with an electric mixer until soft peaks form. Add the granulated white sugar gradually, whisking well with each addition, until glossy and firm. Spoon over the filling to cover it completely. Swirl the meringue into peaks and sprinkle with the golden sugar. Bake for 20 to 30 minutes, or until the meringue is crispy and pale gold but still soft in the center.

Let cool slightly before serving.

Bread and Butter Pudding With Whiskey Sauce

Is there any better fate for a loaf of stale bread than to be turned into this amazing Southern treat? This is the ultimate comfort food dessert, and perfect for a large group.

For the bread pudding...
6 large eggs
1½ cups white granulated sugar
4 cups milk
1 cup heavy cream
1 tbsp bourbon whiskey
1 tbsp vanilla extract
1 tsp ground cinnamon
Pinch of allspice
1 (1 lb) loaf day-old French bread, torn into 1 inch chunks
4 tbsps melted butter
½ cup golden raisins

For the whiskey sauce...
1 cups white sugar
½ cup butter
½ cup corn syrup
¼ cup bourbon whiskey, or to taste

Pre-heat oven to 325°F.

In a mixing bowl, whisk together the eggs and sugar until light and creamy. Add the milk, cream, whiskey, vanilla, cinnamon, and allspice. Whisk thoroughly until combined.

Scatter the bread in a 9 x 13 inch baking dish, and drizzle over the melted butter. Toss until coated. Top with the raisins. Cover with the custard mixture. Let still out for 30 minutes to allow the bread to soak up the custard.

Bake about 40 minutes, or until the custard is set and the top is browned. Let cool for 15 minutes before serving. May be served warm, room temperature, or cold.

To make the sauce: Mix the sugar, butter, and corn syrup in saucepan over low heat. Stir until the butter is melted, the sugar is dissolved, and the mixture is heated through. Whisk in the whiskey. May be served over the bread pudding warm, or at room temperature.

Serves 10

Peach Cobbler

Whenever people do those word association exercises, and the word is "summer", the most common response is, "peach cobbler".

For the filling...
6 peaches, peeled and sliced
4 tbsps sugar
½ tbsp lemon juice
1½ tsp cornstarch
½ tsp almond or vanilla essence
Vanilla or pecan ice cream

For the pie topping...
1½ cups all purpose flour
½ cup granulated white sugar
1½ tsps baking powder
½ tsp salt
6 tbsps diced butter
1 egg
6 tbsps milk

Pre-heat oven to 425°F.

Place the peaches in a 9 inch square ovenproof dish. Add the sugar, lemon juice, cornflour and almond essence and toss together. Bake in pre-heated oven for 20 minutes.

Meanwhile, to make the topping, sift the flour, all but 2 tbsps of the sugar, the baking powder and the salt into a bowl. Rub in the butter with the fingertips until the mixture resembles breadcrumbs. Mix the egg and 5 tbsps of the milk in a jug, then mix into the dry ingredients with a fork until a soft, sticky dough forms. If the dough seems too dry, stir in the extra tbsp of milk.

Reduce the oven temperature to 400°F. Remove the peaches from the oven and drop spoonfuls of the topping over the surface, without smoothing. Sprinkle with the remaining sugar, return to the oven and bake for a further 15 minutes or until the topping is golden brown and firm – the topping will spread as it cooks. Serve hot or at room temperature, with ice cream.

Serves 4-6

Rhubarb Crumble

Rhubarb's unique, tart flavor makes it a great complement for this easy dessert's sweet crumble topping.

2 lb rhubarb
½ cup granulated white sugar
Grated zest and juice of 1 orange
2½ cups plain or wholewheat flour
4 tbsps butter
⅔ cup brown sugar
1 tsp ground ginger
Cream or yogurt, to serve

Pre-heat oven to 375°F.

Cut the rhubarb into 1 inch lengths and place in a 3 pint flameproof dish with the sugar and the orange rind and juice.

Make the crumble by placing the flour in a mixing bowl and rubbing in the butter until the mixture resembles bread crumbs. Stir in the brown sugar and the ginger.

Spread the crumble evenly over the fruit and press down lightly using a fork.

Bake in the centre of the oven on a baking sheet for 25 to 30 minutes until the crumble is golden brown

Serve warm with cream or ice-cream.

Serves 6

Pecan Pie

America's crunchiest pie is the ideal change of pace from all those soft, fruit-filled varieties.

For the pie dough...
1¾ cups all-purpose flour, plus extra for dusting
½ cup butter
2 tbsps granulated white sugar

For the filling...
5 tbsps butter
Scant ½ cup light brown sugar
⅔ cup dark corn syrup
2 extra-large eggs, beaten
1 tsp vanilla extract
1 cup pecans

Pre-heat oven to 400°F.

For the pie dough, place the flour in a bowl and rub in the butter using your fingertips until it resembles fine breadcrumbs. Stir in the granulated white sugar and add enough cold water to mix to a firm dough. Wrap in plastic wrap and chill for 15 minutes, until firm enough to roll out.

Roll out the dough on a lightly-floured counter and use to line a 9 inch round, loose-bottomed tart pan. Prick the bottom with a fork. Chill for 15 minutes.

Place the tart pan on a cookie sheet, line with a sheet of parchment paper, and fill with dried beans. Bake in the pre-heated oven for 10 minutes. Remove the paper and beans and bake for an additional 5 minutes. Reduce the oven temperature to 350°F.

For the filling, place the butter, brown sugar, and corn syrup in a saucepan and heat gently until melted. Remove from the heat and quickly beat in the eggs and vanilla extract.

Coarsely chop the pecans and stir into the mixture. Pour into the tart shell and bake for 35 to 40 minutes, until the filling is just set. Serve warm or cold.

Serves 8

Very Berry Crisp

This super-easy fruit dessert can be made with any combination of berries. Just don't forget to put vanilla ice cream on the grocery list (or better yet, make some homemade).

2 lbs mixed berries – any combo of raspberries, blackberries, strawberries, blueberries, etc., fresh or frozen, thawed
¾ cup granulated white sugar
1 tsp fresh lemon juice
1 tbsp cornstarch
⅛ tsp cinnamon
½ cup flour
½ cup packed brown sugar
⅔ cup quick cooking rolled oats
¼ tsp ground ginger
⅛ tsp salt
4 tbsps cold butter, cut in small pieces

Pre-heat oven to 375°F.

In a bowl combine the berries, granulated sugar, lemon juice, cornstarch, and cinnamon; mix to combine thoroughly. Pour into a lightly-buttered 2 quart baking dish.

In the same bowl combine the flour, brown sugar, oats, ginger, salt, and butter. Using a pastry cutter or your fingertips, cut or rub the butter into the dry ingredients to form a very coarse, crumbly mixture.

Spread the mixture over the berries and bake at 375 °F. for 40 minutes, or until a bubbly, well-browned crust forms.

Let sit for at least 15 minutes, before serving warm with ice cream.

Serves 6-8

Lemon Curd

Lemon curd is delicious and easy to make. It is best eaten fresh but can be stored for upto 2 months in a refrigerator. Use on scones, to make lemon tarts or as a filling for sponge cakes.

3 large lemons washed in hot water
1½ cups of granulated white sugar
3 eggs, beaten
1½ sticks of butter

You will need 2 jam jars or 3 to 4 small jars with lids and waxed discs. To sterilize the jars, make sure they are washed in soapy water and rinsed well and then heat in a moderate oven for 5 minutes.

Carefully grate the rind from each of the lemons using a fine grater. Make sure you only take the yellow rind and not the bitter white pith.

Cut the lemons in half and squeeze out all the juice, then sieve to remove the pips.

Place a medium heatproof bowl over a saucepan of simmering water and add the lemon rind, juice and sugar. Mix together well until the sugar has dissolved.

Add the eggs and the butter cut into small pieces and continue to stir for 25 to 30 minutes until the butter has melted and the mixture begins to thicken. Beat well and turn into the jars. Cover and label before storing. Once opened the lemon curd will keep for up to 2 months in the refrigerator.

Makes 700g

Index

Radishes
Three Bean Salad 48

Rhubarb Crumble 306

Rice
Hoppin' John 126
Jambalaya 80
Stuffed Bell Peppers 148

Roast Turkey Breast With Cranberry Sauce 196
Roasted Artichokes 104
Roasted Red Potato Salad 38
Roasted Vegetables 92

Salad Greens
Caesar Salad With Homemade Garlic Croutons 44
Three Bean Salad 48
Waldorf Salad 34

Salads
Caesar Salad With Homemade Garlic Croutons 44
Cobb Salad 36
Deli-Style Macaroni Salad 42
Potato & Egg Salad 40
Roasted Red Potato Salad 38
Southwest Corn Salad 46
Three Bean Salad 48
Waldorf Salad 34

Salmon
Grilled Salmon Fillet With Fresh Mango Salsa 206
Potato Pancakes With Smoked Salmon & Dill
 Sour Cream 250
Wild Salmon Cakes With Tarragon Aioli 216

Salsa
Avocado Salsa 224
Mango Salsa 206
Tomato Salsa 22

San Francisco Cioppino 220

Sausage
Chicken Fried Steak With Country Cream
 Gravy 138
Chicken & Sausage Gumbo 78
Chorizo & Cheese Quesadillas With Chipotle
 Sour Cream 28
Jambalaya 80
Sausage Mushroom Breakfast Casserole 260
Stuffed Bell Peppers 148

Scalloped Potatoes 120

Shrimp
Chicken & Sausage Gumbo 78
Garlic Shrimp Angel Hair 218
Jambalaya 80
San Francisco Cioppino 220
Shrimp Cocktail 10
Shrimp & Grits 222

Sloppy Joes 134
Slow-Roasted Pulled Pork With Kansas City
 Barbecue Sauce 152
Smothered Pork Chops 162

Soups
Corn & Clam Chowder 68
Cream Of Broccoli Soup With Cheddar Croutons 70
Cream Of Mushroom Soup 56
Cream Of Tomato Soup 64
Easy Gazpacho 52
Garden Vegetable Soup 62
Lobster Bisque 72
Mom's Chicken Noodle Soup 66
New England Clam Chowder 60
Spiced Pumpkin Soup 58
Split Pea With Ham 54

Southwest Corn Salad 46
Spaghetti & Meatballs 164
Spice-Rubbed Seared Tuna Steaks With
 Balsamic Reduction 204
Spiced Pumpkin Soup 58

Spinach
Baked Spinach & Feta Omelet 252
Garden Vegetable Soup 62
Halibut Steaks With Spinach & Warm
 Bacon Dressing 210
Oyster Rockefeller 26
Spinach Artichoke Dip 24
Steakhouse Creamed Spinach 102

Split Pea With Ham Soup 54

Squash
Baked Acorn Squash 116

Steakhouse Creamed Spinach 102

Stews
Chicken & Sausage Gumbo 78
"Chili Verde" Green Pork Stew 76
Hearty Beef Stew 74
Jambalaya 80

Sticky Ginger Garlic Wings 20
Succulent Succotash 98
Sweet Potato Pie 296

Texas Lone Star Chili 84
Three Bean Salad 48

Tomatoes
Chicken Parmesan Casserole With Tomato Sauce 176
Chicken & Sausage Gumbo 78
Chicken & White Bean Chili 86
Cobb Salad 36
Crab Fritters With Avocado Salsa 224
Cream Of Tomato Soup 64
Easy Gazpacho 52
Firehouse Chili Con Carne 82
Fresh Tomato Salsa 22
Garden Vegetable Soup 62
Garlic Shrimp Angel Hair 218
Halibut Steaks With Spinach & Warm
Bacon Dressing 210
Hunter's Chicken 178
Jambalaya 80
King Ranch Chicken Casserole 188
Oyster Po' Boys 226
San Francisco Cioppino 220
Spaghetti & Meatballs 164
Stuffed Bell Peppers 148
Succulent Succotash 98
Texas Lone Star Chili 84
Three Bean Salad 48

Tortillas
Chorizo & Cheese Quesadillas With Chipotle
 Sour Cream 28
King Ranch Chicken Casserole 188

Tuna
Classic Tuna Noodle Casserole 228
Spice-Rubbed Seared Tuna Steaks With
 Balsamic Reduction 204

Turkey
Roast Turkey Breast With Cranberry Sauce 196
Turkey Cutlets 198

Vanilla Ice Cream With Chocolate Sauce 294
Very Berry Crisp 310

Waldorf Salad 34

Walnuts
Banana Nut Bread 242
Carrot Cake With Cream Cheese Frosting 268
Chocolate Chip Cookies 270
Chocolate Walnut Fudge 276
Cinnamon Swirl Sour Cream Bundt Cake 282
Double Fudge Brownies 278
Waldorf Salad 34

Watercress
Oyster Rockefeller 26

Whoopie Pies 288

Yams, Glazed 112
Yankee Pot Roast 136

Zucchini
Garden Vegetable Soup 62
Roasted Vegetables 92
Succulent Succotash 98